D1125831

FREEDOM

FREEDOM
The Story of My Second Life

MALIKA OUFKIR
Translated by Linda Coverdale

miramax books

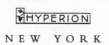

NEW YORK

ISBN 1-4013-5206-5

First Edition
10   9   8   7   6   5   4   3   2   1

To the memory of
Saïda Mnebhi

CONTENTS

Contents

1
ADAM

Adam. My little Adam, my love, my life. It took me all this time, all these trials and tribulations, to awaken to myself, and finally accept who I am. At my age, when so many women face a change of life, I am instead finally coming into my own as a normal woman who, although unable to give life, can at least save one. For Adam might easily have died, and no one would ever have known. Instead, he is the child of a miracle.

On the second floor of the League for Child Welfare, bathed in the clear light of Marrakesh, my throat tightens at the cloying smells of milk, sugar, medicine, and diapers. We are all equals here. A smiling woman in strict Islamic dress is playing with a baby only two steps away from a Spanish woman who has been waiting weeks for a child. I have come to adopt a girl, and I'm lucky: there's one available. An adorable curly-haired girl, the only one among some thirty boys who are crying, whimpering, or peacefully sleeping. She's so quiet. She was probably hoping I would come. I take her in my arms, but I don't understand: I feel nothing. Why this utter absence of emotion? It's terrible, unfair. I get goosebumps. My intuition tells me that this little girl with black eyes will not be my child. Standing tensely on the threshold of the most important moment of my life, I study the newborns through the protective glass of their cradles. My mother, Fatima Oufkir, has come along with me, and now she holds out a tiny ball of brown hair and wrinkles.

She says, quite simply, "Here is your son."

How can she be so certain?

"I don't know, Mama," I say, "it's a boy."

"Yes, your boy," she insists.

Gently, I pick up this tiny being who, at two weeks, weighs barely six pounds, and the deepest part of my being comes alive with a joy mingled with pain and fear. In a single moment I feel all the heartrending rewards of motherhood.

Adam is a gift from heaven, because heaven spared him. Like most children who end up at the League, he was probably abandoned at the hospital in Marrakesh by a mother too poor to nurse him. I would learn later that in June 2005, during the worst heat of the summer, an old beggarwoman had been carrying him under her armpit like a bundle of dirty rags, almost stifling him. Accustomed to such pitiful sights, the police followed the wretched woman and rescued the child, whose photo was then posted in all the precincts of Marrakesh, to give his mother a chance to come forward. She never did.

In July 2005, Eric and I decided to adopt the child I would name Adam. After much administrative protocol, for adoption as practiced in the West is outlawed by Islamic law, he would bear my name—that is to say, my father's: Oufkir. It was my way of remembering where I came from. I needed this baby, and I gave him that last name, to wipe out all my pain, to forget the murderers who stole twenty years of my life, making me feel I would forever be a victim, robbing me of the inalienable gift of childbearing—that grace all women possess—and leaving me diminished, as if a part of me had been cut off. I had suffered so much from being unable to have a child with Eric that we had sometimes come close to separating. I didn't want to be a victim any longer, or to have a message for the world. I wanted to go on with my life, and not simply have survived my past.

The road forward had been long and difficult. I was already the legal guardian of my niece Nawal, whom I loved like a daughter and who lived with me in Miami. But Nawal had real parents. Then something happened, and everything changed.

As fate would have it, my dear friend Soundous, whom I'd met when she was in Morocco working for Pharmacists Without Borders, underwent an operation for cancer of the uterus in February 2005, at the Pierre and Marie Curie Hospital in Paris. It was because she'd wanted a child that her doctors had discovered her uterine sarcoma.

Death is, at every moment, so close to us. I slept beside Soundous every night, and as she spoke to me about the possibility of adoption, I found myself slowly persuaded by her words. Eric's love, his generosity and patience, also brought me closer to the unknown child who would one day be placed into my arms. I waited ten years before deciding to become a mother, ten years before accepting that there really was a freedom I could call my own, a destiny that belonged only to me.

Freedom: the word was foreign to me, and naturally it tasted strange—even bitter—on my tongue. From the palace of Mohammed V, where I had been an untouchable princess, to the vile prison where I'd played Scheherazade to my attentive family, when had I not been a prisoner?

Barriers, real and invisible, are all around us, especially in our own heads. But if there's one thing a prisoner has, it's time to think, and when I moved to France, after my imprisonment in Morocco, I slowly learned the often painful lessons of freedom. Now, as I begin my third life, I have understood this much: love is all there is. The love you give, the love you receive. And the story of my apprenticeship in freedom will reveal how I finally embraced this simple truth.

2
FREEDOM

It is July 16, 1996, and in a few hours the bulky 747 will descend through the clouds, and at long last I will breathe the air of freedom. Somewhere thirty thousand feet below me, my true love, my family, friends, and a new life are waiting for me, as if those twenty-four years of confinement had been nothing but a bad dream. The sky is blue, almost unbelievably blue, and I feel so far away. The Moroccan coastline recedes; already Spain appears. How many years it's taken me to get here, to reach this moment, alone among strangers, in this deafening aircraft!

It all began in 1958, when a little girl was brought to the palace on the orders of Mohammed V, descendant of the Prophet and the Alaouite dynasty, to be raised as a princess and playmate beside his daughter Lalla Amina, cherished child of the King and Lalla Bahia, his favorite concubine. My first name means "Little Queen" in Arabic. Until that day I had been the "little queen" of my father, Mohammed Oufkir, but now I became an adopted princess, the sad and mischievous jester to a medieval court where concubines spied on one another, where harems closed their ranks on the dark eyes of the King's favorite, where the "fire slaves," whose job was to administer corporal punishment, were unsparing with the lash.

It was my rebellious temperament that made me resist the strict regime of Jeanne Rieffel, the Alsatian governess recommended to the King by the Comte de Paris. Her big blue eyes never missed a thing, and this authoritarian spinster, who hated men and disdained the pleasures of life, raised us with an iron rod. Still, I can't forget the laughter I shared with Lalla Amina, the carriage rides, the palace with its enormous patios, the private ski trails at Ifrane. I was torn between East and West, speaking French with my parents and Arabic at the palace; expressions from the old-fashioned and highly refined dialect used at court made their way permanently into my speech. Wherever I go in Morocco, I am still asked if I belong to *Dar-el-Mahzran*: the house of power. But I was no princess, and the next years of my life, spent in a foul jail, would confirm this.

I bridled then, and still do, at all forms of authority. Even during my golden childhood, utterly free of care, revolt smoldered in my heart. I didn't want my past to be denied, even then! When the royal court adopted you, it cut you off from your roots, doing its best to convince you that you had no other family. The harem was full of women without any identity, anonymous souls who would end their lives sadly, alone and wrinkled, though their beds had once been honored by the

King. When Mohammed V died in 1961, his son Hassan II became king, and of course I loved this new adopted father, stern and mocking, who later turned savagely against me and my kin. Yet I wanted to leave: I was a prisoner and I knew it. I had a family whom I wanted to see again.

Sometimes, when I tell this story that is so much like a fairy tale, I get the impression people don't believe me. Abducting a girl of five from her parents? It might seem cruel, but it would have been impossible for my parents to refuse the wish of a monarch whose hand one kissed, kneeling, upon entering his presence. At the time, my father was only a soldier, and not yet the second most powerful man in the kingdom, answering only to the King himself. Married on June 29, 1952, to the ever-so-pretty fifteen-year-old Fatima Chenna, my father, Mohammed Oufkir, was seventeen years older than my mother. He was born on September 29, 1920, at Ain-Chair in the Tafilalet region, stronghold of the Berbers of the Atlas Mountains in Morocco. His name, Oufkir, means "the impoverished."

At the age of seven he lost his father, Ahmed Oufkir, chief of his village and later appointed pasha—provincial governor—of Bou-Denib by Marshal Lyautey, then resident general under the French protectorate. The army soon became my father's only family. He was indisputably brilliant. At the age of twenty-one, he enlisted as a reserve second lieutenant in the French army. He was wounded in Italy, earned his captain's stripes in Indochina, and was soon named chief aide-de-camp to Mohammed V. When Hassan II came to power on March 3, 1961, my father won the new King's trust. When Mehdi Ben Barka, leader of the Moroccan opposition and founder of the Union Nationale des Forces Populaires, was kidnapped outside the Brasserie Lipp in the middle of Saint-Germain des Prés in 1965, my father was suspected of involvement, and the French sentenced him *in absentia* to life in prison.

He was Minister of the Interior then. People spoke of him as omnipotent, and for all intents and purposes he was. Unfortunately, the regime he served was undermined by corruption, the exercise of arbitrary power, and the pomp of a King to whom the West gave its complete support.

Then came the Skhirat coup. One beautiful day in July 1971, more than a thousand soldiers led by two NCOs from the royal military training college burst into the palace at Skhirat during the King's birthday celebrations. They massacred almost a hundred guests while the King hid in the bathroom. My father was loyal to the King but also to the army, his foster family, even in revolt; he pleaded successfully for the lives of the 1,081 rebel trainee officers, but the harshness of subsequent reprisals left my father a changed man. He grew melancholy and dreamed of starting over in a simpler, more austere life.

Never had he held so much power in his hands: he had been named Minister of Defense and head of the royal air force. A beautiful wife, six children, a career that had led him to the summit of state power, the charisma of a handsome soldier with a commanding presence: he had it all. He was to lose it all, including his life.

I had a friend, Mina, who was the daughter of General Med-bouh, who had been assassinated by his accomplice Colonel Ababou at Skhirat. Out of panic, or a perfectly understandable fear of further trouble with the state, Mina changed her name. I remember the decision shocked me at the time. Whatever happens to me in my life, I told myself, I'll always keep my own name: Oufkir. In Morocco, as elsewhere, my name invoked fear and respect, and opened doors to a life of extraordinary privilege. But this very name would later plunge me into hell.

In 1972, I was in Paris, studying—after a fashion—for my baccalaureate, going out every night, and a spoiled teenager I would have remained had it not been for the car accident that nearly cost me an eye. The doctors saved it, but the operation left scars, and later in prison I often suffered facial tics. I had to return to Morocco to convalesce. I planned to resit my exams in December, since I'd been unable to take them in June.

Events decided otherwise.

My family was spending the summer holidays by the sea, in Kabila. The rift between my father and the King was deeper than ever, and my father was behaving oddly, erratically. I remember him, one minute glum and scanning the horizon, then abruptly singing, dancing, cracking jokes. He took water-skiing lessons, looking ridiculous in his bulky life jacket. He had never been good at displays of affection, but one morning he took me tenderly into his arms, gazing at me intently. Did he already know what awaited him?

On August 16, 1972, I was at home, in the living room of our house in Casablanca, when I turned on the television and heard a reporter announce there had just been a coup d'état. The royal plane had been fired on over Tétouan. There was no word yet about who was behind the attack. I just lay there, frantic, not knowing what to do. At three the next morning, my grandfather called and asked me to come home to Rabat. I refused. Then at five my mother called and bluntly announced: "Your father's dead. Pack your things and come back to Rabat."

I couldn't understand. I refused to believe in the reality of it all until the horrible moment when I saw my father's body, washed and laid out in a white *jellaba,* a scornful smile on his lips, as if in defiance of death. As though in a nightmare, I could picture the bullet holes in his body: one in the liver, one in the lungs, one in the belly, one in the back, and the last, the death wound, in the neck. The official verdict was suicide. How did one commit suicide with five bullets? This spineless lie only presaged the greater cowardice of what was to come.

My father had been "the most loyal among the loyal." He had committed treason by leading the conspiracy, and the King's rage would now fall upon us. When did family ties become a crime? Why should children be made to pay for what their parents do? I could not forgive my adopted father, Hassan II, for murdering my father. I hated him for maiming the childhoods of my brothers and sisters. I hated him because we were all innocent children.

Stunned, I saw myself thrown into a cell like a criminal with my mother; my sisters Soukaina, Myriam, and Maria; my brothers Raouf and Abdellatif, the youngest of us all, only three at the time; Achoura Chenna, our governess and Mother's first cousin, who was a year older than her; and Halima Boudi, Abdellatif's governess, who was my own age. Hapless, helpless victims who chose to share our fate.

"Mademoiselle, would you like a drink?"

The smiling stewardess bending toward me to offer refreshment has no idea of the hell from which I have returned. How could she, seeing me here, imagine that where I once lived, orange juice in a plastic cup had been the peak of luxury? In *Stolen Lives*, I recounted the conditions of our imprisonment: people believed we were living in comfort, simply kept under surveillance, at worst, but I try to picture the faces of our friends—all the hangers-on who had flocked to my parents' table—if they'd known that fleas bit our legs until they bled, mice robbed us of the few scraps of food we had, and rats ran along our limbs at night, not to mention the scorpions and the infernal desert locusts.

How can I forget my attempts at suicide? The molesting hands of drunken inmates, for whom we were fresh meat? The despair, the surprise inspections by soldiers as brutal as they were stupid, the arrogance of petty wardens? How did we manage to hold on? Perhaps because we were a family, perhaps because we clung to a bit of humor, even in the depths of horror. Surely because we did not give up hope, despite having been buried alive.

For a long time after I was freed I remained in a prison of

my own mind, a depressed and fearful recluse. Time did not pass for me as for others: every minute was long, threatening, unsettled. I had a distorted sense of time that, even today, keeps me from being on time for my appointments. I lagged twenty years behind the modern world. Without the radio we hid at every search, we would have known nothing of the world outside. When we dug a tunnel with our bare hands, when I rediscovered daylight, cars, men, the wild beauty of my country, I hated more than ever the lackeys of the despot who had robbed us of our precious youth. We were extraterrestrials, Martians in exile on planet Earth. As far as I was concerned, this explained things perfectly. I remained a Martian for a long time.

After our much-publicized escape, which brought our torturers their turn at being tortured, we were a problem for the King. He could neither get rid of us nor set us free in front of the reporters' microphones. Instead, we were put in a villa, surrounded by high walls, in Targa, a favorite vacation spot for the Casablancan bourgeoisie a few kilometers from Marrakesh. We were not allowed to leave. We would wake at night with a start, haunted by ghosts of the past or a sudden devastating hunger. We still hoped to obtain, through our French lawyers, a visa for Canada, of whose cool breezes we had dreamed on many a sleepless night spent rotting away in jail. Now we were really dreaming! We were emotionally and sexually frustrated because even our limited new freedom had released feelings and desires long stifled by prison, forcing us to transfer our need for love onto our ten cats and two dogs.

Then suddenly, out of the blue, we were told: "You're free! Leave the house!" Was it too good to be true?

On February 26, 1991, in jeans and a man's shirt, I took my first steps into the outside world. Alas, for over five years we would now be watched and followed, our phones tapped at every turn. Potential employers were discouraged from giving us jobs. Our friends, flirtations, and even lovers were interrogated by Home Security, the Moroccan secret service. Freedom? No, I had simply been released into a much larger prison, one where I had to make my way on my own, even though I no longer knew how. I had to relearn everything. I had trouble with the notion of time, not knowing when I had to hurry and when I had time to spare, not understanding the imperatives of schedules. I had difficulty decoding social customs. My heart was heavy. The word "happiness" had been banished from my vocabulary. I no longer knew how to be the haughty beauty who'd partied her eighteenth birthday away at a splendid ball. Who was Malika Oufkir? Someone else.

With neither fixed address nor work permit, I was a phantom. Although I was able to land a job through sheer tenacity and the courage of Noureddine Ayouche, the head of Shem's advertising agency, I slunk through life. Even today, I'm still a ghost, though the ball and chain I trail are now invisible.

In two hours, I'll be reunited with my sister Maria, whose escape from Morocco to Spain by sea on June 25, 1996, set me on the road to the new life I have now. It was she who first roused public opinion in France; it's to her that I owe my passport and the very fact that I am here on this plane, heading for the free world. I'm forty-three years old and at long last, everything is beginning for me.

The flight from Rabat to Paris in this enormous machine buffeted by the winds has felt like an eternity. All around me I see dozens of sullen strangers strapped into their seats, and the uniformed flight attendants' smiles seem strained. Sometimes our invisible captain speaks to us in a tinny voice, like the unseen impresario of a bizarre puppet show in which all these people are playing their parts with practiced ease. Alone, lost in my seat as if I were floating out in mid-ocean, I shiver to think that someone might stare at me, size me up, pass judgment on me. I am an outsider in this world of free men and women, a world I left behind so long ago that I have forgotten how to blend into it unnoticed. A feeling of oppression overwhelms me, flooding my entire body. Through the porthole I watch the endless movie of a limitless sky, too vast for the human eye.

At last the final door to freedom opens. A narrow plastic tunnel leads from the plane to the arrival area. Emerging from that telescopic corridor, I recognize my sister's face, lost in a sea of cameras, photographers, and waving microphones. I am bombarded with camera flashes and stupid questions. What are you feeling right now? What is it like to feel free? Do you have any plans? What will you do tomorrow? Have you anything to say?

I have so many things to say, but I forgot long ago how to talk to other people. I have lived as a young woman of good family, a princess, and a prisoner. It's so hard to sum all that up in a few words! And besides, my past does not interest the avid pack of reporters pressing in around me, because they want drama, and they want it now: tales of tragedy, misery, tears. For the moment, all I have to give them is the mute spectacle of my distress. And nothing more.

I advance unseeing, mechanically. Suddenly the man of my life steps over a barrier, lifts me up, and carries me off. My first vision of Paris is in Eric's arms.

3

ERIC

Who am I? The woman being bundled off in this car? The woman recently emancipated by a king's whim, like a slave in this modern-day world? Today, July 16, 1996, the sky is blue. I should be filled with joy at returning to the city where I had so much fun as a student. Life should reassert itself, but nothing happens. Instead, I'm empty, numb, struck dumb. My heart has been so deeply hurt that it's incapable of feeling. I need a defibrillator. From time to time, in moments darker than ever before, I fear that I'll never be able to love again.

My brother Raouf and my sister Soukaina have been freed as well, and we all gather at the home of one of my mother's sisters. We hug; we breathe the air of freedom. Yet I feel far away from myself. Only after reaching Eric's Parisian apartment, getting past a keypad code, a gate, and a door, do I realize that I am still in prison, inside my head. I have become my own jailer. Without Eric's infinite patience and unstinting support, I would have surely collapsed.

I met Eric Bordreuil in Morocco in the spring of 1995. Deprived of both a passport and civil rights after my family's release from prison, I had thrown myself headlong into work. I'd first found employment thanks to Noureddine Ayouche, who hired me to assist him as a production manager at his advertising agency. I wasn't going out much, and when I did, it was for entirely professional reasons, so I should logically have declined the invitation of my friends Myriam and Kamil Ben Jelloun to attend their wedding, with its inevitable procession of dolled-up women dripping with jewels, and all the ostentation that made me feel so uncomfortable. But Myriam had asked for my help, and I couldn't say no—and if I had turned my friends down, I would never have met Eric.

On the very morning of the *hammam* ceremony attended by the bride and her friends, I got a phone call from one of my good friends, who is something of a clairvoyant.

She told me breathlessly: "Kika, you've met him, the man from across the sea, the man of your life."

What foolishness! I didn't believe a word of it. Besides, I wasn't free to love whom I chose, since Home Security systematically interrogated anyone who came near me. I went no farther with foreigners than accompanying them to their planes. Each encounter gave me the feeling of being trapped in a deep-sea diving bell, watching the world from the well of my solitude.

When, seated beside me at the wedding banquet, I saw a

tall, smiling, dark-haired man with mischievous brown eyes, when I understood moreover that he spoke fluent Arabic, I let myself be carried away. Where did this fragile feeling of hope come from? What if he were the one? It wasn't love at first sight. It was more like a feeling of safety spreading through me, a slow warmth, followed by a growing emotional bond.

I was frightened, of course; it took years for my deep-seated fears to disappear. For one year, during which Eric was searched, watched, and followed by the authorities, he came to see me every Friday night, and when he left I was overcome with feelings of abandonment. He had the patience to stand by me while I recovered, and to tame the little girl masquerading as a middle-aged woman, the lover who forbade herself pleasure out of guilt. He understood me from the inside out.

One day I told him: "You are only European on the outside. Inside, you have an oriental heart. You're an easterner, Eric."

Hailing from an old Protestant family with roots in Nîmes and the Ardèche, Eric inherited his patient tolerance from his parents, who are extraordinary people. Pierre Bordreuil, his father, is an archaeologist at the National Center for Scientific Research (Centre National de Recherches Scientifiques); I nicknamed him "Find-it-all." He was a man sometimes unbelievably consumed by his passion for his work. Though born in Strasbourg, Eric was only three when his family moved, for the sake of his father's research, first to East Jerusalem and then to Lebanon, where Eric grew up. My mother-in-law, Françoise, was the principal of the Collège Protestant Français in Beirut.

What a woman! Her courage and intellectual honesty led her to play a modest role during the civil war in Lebanon, when various Christian and Muslim factions fought for control of the country. She even opened her high school to Palestinians; Arafat's brother found refuge there. When she came to Marrakesh to meet the woman who had stolen her son, I used all my charms to win her to my side. After all, I was only eleven years her junior. She was familiar with my story, and she knew that on the road to recovery, nothing comes easily.

Eric and I were married on October 10, 1998, before a few close friends at the town hall of the 13th arrondissement of Paris. And that was the whole affair: two witnesses, a wedding on the fly. The lack of ceremony was held against me, a bit. But was I capable of anything more extravagantly planned, less improvised? I'd accomplished the main thing: getting Eric to propose.

I've put Eric to the test many times over, goading him to leave me because I could never bear him a child, feeling guilty for not being an ideal wife set on carrying on his name. I skirted the edge of the abyss, then, staying in bed for hours on end, staring into nothing, unable even to watch TV. On our first trip together, in 1996, we had gone to the Ivory Coast to visit one of his best friends, who is an architect like Eric. We stayed in the Hôtel Ivoire, one of the best hotels in Abidjan, and the place seemed a paradise in every way. Yet I stepped away from all the warmth, alone, onto the balcony. I couldn't talk to anyone or share my feelings.

I gazed at the lush African foliage and suddenly called out to God, asking Him, "Why have you given me this freedom?

Why did you rescue me from my cell if I no longer have the heart to live?"

Eric would help me as, feeling my way along, I found my way back to my life. He would encourage me to shed my anonymity, to step out from the shadows I've always hated, to make my voice heard. I had a mission, he said. I was not a nobody. He would encourage me to tell the world about the horrors my family suffered for twenty years. I had a mission, and I would accomplish it with *Stolen Lives*.

But all the time I was working on my first book, daily life in my new Parisian home went on. Going out, eating, sleeping. Putting one foot in front of the other.

"Get dressed, we're going out to dinner!" Did I forget to mention that Eric has a good appetite? Alas, I no longer get much pleasure from food.

The last time I had dined at La Coupole, the famous brasserie in Montparnasse, was in 1972. Dining there is more than merely eating—it's being in the know, in the flow, in the show, just like in the good old days, in the Paris of my youth. When Eric planned our first night out as lovers, he knew that by taking me there, he would realize one of my most cherished dreams.

Has he anticipated my absolute silence, an emptiness so chilling that my very bones grow cold and words freeze in my throat? I doubt it, but there we sit at our table, where I struggle in vain to overcome this numbness. The ballet of white-jacketed waiters, the shining trays they carry aloft, the hum of conversation, the warm colors, the lights . . . This is the world of freedom, and it exhausts me, eating me up from inside. Perhaps it's just too soon, or maybe I'll stay broken forever. La Coupole is like all those things one idealizes for so long that they lose their true meaning. The place belonged to me in my dreams, where I had dined there many a time, re-creating from memory a phantom restaurant that I cannot find anywhere this evening.

After dinner, my fatigue gives way to dread when I notice the maître d' going around the dining room, carefully verifying each check. He carries a strange little machine that he seems to use at each table. Black thoughts swoop down on me, fears of being arrested. Trembling, I reach for Eric's hand.

"Careful, I think they're looking for someone. Some kind of con man, maybe. Look, they're examining all the checks."

Before Eric can reply, the maître d' starts toward us, bringing his little box. Smiling to reassure me, Eric hands him a credit card that the man slips into his machine. For a few seconds of silence, I breathlessly await the verdict. At last the box creaks out a receipt, while Eric returns the card to his pocket.

"Thank you, sir."

Dumbfounded, I watch the maître d' walk off with his miraculous box. If a little piece of plastic slipped into a box can buy a lavish platter of seafood, then the world I once knew is truly dead.

Some time later, searching for my lost identity, I return on my own to Saint Germain des Prés, a neighborhood I used to know well. Instead of destroying my personality, prison preserved it, reshaping it a little, perhaps, but at least I never forgot who I really was. But now freedom has stripped me of my identity as a prisoner and made me one of those thousands of anonymous figures wandering through the streets of Paris. The outside world empties me out, and I feel like a handful of sand cast to the wind.

I still remember the 1970s, though, and the carefree girl I used to be, and today I have come looking for that ghost in all my favorite places: the café terraces of the Latin Quarter, the pricey shops of the Place Saint Sulpice . . . I walk along the Boulevard Saint Germain in a daze, lost in a whirl of memories. Here I am in a Left Bank boutique, Yves Saint Laurent, as if I were still an important general's daughter with her head in the clouds, living in luxury and ease. And for just one second, I can almost believe that I only imagined those years of darkness, and that time actually stood still in this store a whole lifetime ago. Except for one little thing: I'm no longer that smug girl of eighteen, so sure of her charm, with long, wavy hair and a tiny miniskirt, admiring herself in the mirrors as she walks by. Those candy pinks and turquoise blues of another era feel so distant now, outdated not only like the dresses they adorned but, above all, like my desire to blend in. The somber earth tones of the clothes I'm wearing now—the browns, grays, and ochers—speak volumes about the time I've spent far away from this boutique.

"May I help you, madame? We also have that model in black."

The saleswoman's artificial politeness jolts me back to reality, and I panic. Confused and ashamed, I put back the garment I was holding—and I lie. Pretend I have to check with my husband.

I have never returned to that boutique, which may still be haunted by the ghost of the girl I once was, but if there really were some way to erase the past, I think I would have discovered it a long time ago.

As the days go by, I study the merry-go-round of daily life in the free world. Everyone obediently spends Monday to Friday imprisoned in their offices without trying to escape. On Saturday, their free day, the gates swing open and the herds rush out to shop, because it's time to stock up like sheep on everything and anything, plundering the stores for enough goods to last through the following week. Eric wants to make me a "responsible" person, someone who can join the throng of happy shopping natives. He knows how hard this will be on me, how painful I find it to be among crowds, but we both know that the path to recovery lies through the supermarket, and finally, reluctantly, I go off to the store with him. Sooner or later, I'll be able to go on my own. He says this so often I almost end up believing him.

I will never forget my first visit to that Ali Baba's cave of consumer goods: an ocean of products, colors, music, sounds. Food is just everywhere, overflowing from freezers, piled in heaps, pyramids, neat cubes. The harsh glare reveals whole kilometers of fresh produce, cans, bags . . . absolutely everything and more. It's magical, and yet sickening.

For most of my life, I have been deprived of even vital necessities, and now I'm staring at an endless vision of superfluity. Butter . . . Butter! I used to hoard the tiniest bit of it in a scrap of newspaper, and here there is an entire refrigerated case for butter alone. Sweet, salted, low-sodium, Normandy, reduced fat, whipped, unpasteurized . . . There's so much of it I'm dizzy. Dozens of brands, all packaged differently, from simple foil wrappings to plastic tubs, all brightly colored in red, silver, and gold. And the milk! Also in a hundred forms: whole, skim, 1%, 2%, condensed, evaporated, in cans, bottles, plastic jugs . . . Petrified, I don't dare touch this abundant merchandise, once so sacred and so scarce during my twenty years in purgatory, only a four-hour flight away.

"Take what you want," Eric urges me.

What do I want? I am simply incapable of wanting anything, and I certainly can't take anything. Reaching out for these treasures would paralyze me. If I even touched a bar of butter, I'd be afraid security guards would drag me back to prison as a thief. All around me, the Saturday puppet-people are shamelessly helping themselves, casually grabbing things they barely glance at before tossing them into their shopping carts.

When my astonishment wears off, I am seized with a feeling of outrage: what happens to all these perishable things if they are not sold in time? I can't believe there are enough stomachs in Paris to eat up even half these dairy products. What will happen to this stack of butter packs, obviously untouched, possibly because the red cow adorning the wrapper is less attractive than the one on a rival brand? Eric doesn't know what to say. Maybe they throw the stuff away, or put it on sale; what does it matter, since it's right here? Could even one of these avid shoppers all around me ever understand that just a few years ago, a simple pat of butter would have thrilled me to pieces? Then we're caught up in a tangle of shopping carts, reaching back to the aisles, that reminds me of the unnerving traffic jams of Paris, and I feel so faint I have to sit down.

Twice, I went back to the supermarket with Eric. Twice, I looked at the merchandise but kept my distance, not daring to touch anything. The third time, on his suggestion, I return alone, determined to do it, to fill my shopping cart myself and line up at the checkout, just an ordinary person, lost in the crowd. I push my empty cart around for a few minutes, slowing down in front of some products, passing in front of them two or three times. I feel like a respectable family man afraid to approach a prostitute. Suddenly, something gives way. I start grabbing things. Everything, feverishly. Everything, that is, that I needed and didn't have during all those years in prison. And I'm not interested in low-this or reduced-that, no half measures for me. I go all out: my cart fills up like magic with cleaning supplies, oil, butter, detergent. I buy two of everything—generic dishwashing liquid, even ordinary corn flakes—just in case. In case we run out. Surrounded by all that merchandise, it's hard to believe that anyone could run out of anything, but you never know. As a woman passes me with a child sitting in her cart, I catch her glancing furtively at mine, which seems loaded to stock a survival bunker for World War Three instead of a small family kitchen.

While I am wondering what that woman must be thinking, I happen to notice some packages of cheese on sale. Boursin with garlic, and with herbs: ten little containers for the price of five. Looking around, I realize that luckily, no one else has noticed this amazing opportunity. What a bargain, it's all half-price. Who cares whether it's plain or with garlic, herbs, or paprika—it's an incredible deal, just look at the price tag. Quickly, before anyone beats me to it, I slip three ten-packs into my cart. Thirty little Boursins! I march off proudly, hoping the checkout personnel won't think I have been too selfish and take some away from me.

Home again, I cram my packages of Boursin into our tiny fridge, stashing the treats I'm really fond of way in the back to make them hard to find. It's an old reflex I will probably have a hard time letting go of: protecting what belongs to me, because it might vanish in an instant.

And now I wait, rather pleased with myself, for the return of the man I love, so that I can show off my spoils.

"What's with all the Boursin?" Eric asks, taken aback.

"It was on sale," I tell him. "Guess how much I paid!"

When he smiles, I realize that I have not quite mastered the Saturday Shopping Puppet Show. And the fridge door swings quietly closed on thirty little containers of cheese.

4
FEAR

P arked in front of the building is a white van, its blinking emergency signals flashing orange light across the facade. The driver, his back to me, is unlocking the rear doors of the vehicle, probably to unload the inevitable "shopping," those cardboard boxes packed with provisions and useless items.

Who is he, the man with the van? A neighbor? A delivery guy? He's a stocky little man with a short neck, a bald pate, and middle-aged spread. He doesn't see me, and as I approach him, I worry that he might suddenly turn around, ask me a question, wave, smile at me. This isn't the first time I have come home by myself, but until now I have managed to avoid running into anyone. Except for a matronly lady who ventured to nod at me. For one endless minute, I wonder what I should do, whether I should wait for him to unload the van before I go inside the building . . . How much time will he need? Five minutes, maybe more. But I must get over such anxieties and learn to live with other people. After hesitating for a few seconds, I walk on, determined to brave the usual courtesies.

The man has opened the back of the van, which contains not the expected provisions, but three big dogs, barking piteously. It must be stifling in the van, and the animals are probably yapping to show how happy they are to be free. I know how that feels; in fact, I feel closer to those dogs than I have felt to any person besides Eric. And the van's rear window is protected by a gate with bars, the door to a temporary prison through which the animals have watched an inaccessible Paris slip by: parks, trees, small patches of grass, the modest heaven of city dogs.

The barking seems to bother the man, who starts shouting so loudly he sometimes drowns out all three dogs.

"That's enough! Shut up!"

The noise stops me in my tracks, a few yards from the van. That is when the scene shifts to horror: snatching up a stick, the driver begins to beat his dogs, swinging powerfully, with unbridled violence. The barking turns to whimpering and pitiful little moans; one of the dogs wails at such a high pitch that it sounds like the cry of a newborn baby. The van is abruptly filled with pain, and the man is still hitting them, with sickening energy, bathed in the glare of his blinking emergency lights—in this case, aptly named indeed.

So: when people are free, they can inflict pain for no good reason, heedlessly, with impunity. Unable to bear the whimpering of the poor animals any longer, torn between fear and outrage, I find myself walking stiffly over to the van. The man whips around and glares at me in disbelief, still holding the stick.

"What do *you* want? My picture?"

No, God forbid! Just the sight of his face appalls me, and will haunt me for a long time. With sweat pouring down his cheeks, he brandishes the stick like a blackjack and threatens me in a low voice.

"Nothin' to see here, so move it . . ."

For one instant, I hesitate. With everything that is in me, I want to snatch away his weapon and throw it far beyond his reach, I want to free the dogs, put an end to this torture session. But fear grips me—the fear not of being hit, but of being arrested, interrogated, locked up for meddling in someone else's business. Perhaps this man would have the right to call the police, to file a complaint, and have me taken away. So I stare at him, one last time, before abandoning the dogs to their fate.

"I told you to move it!"

Quaking from head to toe, I go into the building and shut the front door behind me. I feel dirty. Outside, the barking starts up again. And I cannot help imagining this man in the comfort of his own home, dealing out caresses or blows as the mood takes him.

"People call the cops for that," Eric told me.

"People" means "me." I could have. It seems that one can report a free man who beats his dogs. The penalty is often insignificant—a small fine—but the dogs may sometimes be taken away from their tormenter. Then what happens to them? No one can tell me. They are probably sent to an animal shelter. To the SPCA. Where they will wait, in cages, for another free person to come adopt them. For a child to make a choice: Mama, I want the little white doggie. Or for their guardians, unable to feed them for the rest of their lonely days, to decide to give them their last shot, their passport to a better world.

Even if I had known, if I had wanted to, I probably would not have been able to call the police that evening, or any other evening. Uniforms terrify me. They represent the law, authority, brute force. Prison. Those men and women who stroll around with such impressive hardware on their belts (revolvers, handcuffs, clubs, spray cans of mace) are a constant threat to me.

Over time, I've developed actual strategies for eluding the vigilance of people in uniforms. If they are not watching you carefully or have not even noticed you yet, you can casually cross the street, which is what I usually do, holding my breath, hoping not to hear a shrill whistle that would stop me dead in my tracks.

"Hey, you there!"

I can already see myself, frozen in the middle of the street, terror-stricken, hands in the air. The camera zooms in melodramatically: *Midnight Express*, the Parisian version.

When I see no other way out, I go straight to the authorities, perhaps to allay their suspicions, perhaps to put an end
to my wrenching fear: if they want me, let them arrest me, I'm
tired of running. That is why I must have gone up to more than
half the police officers of Paris under the most ridiculous pre-
texts: unnerved by my anxiety, I ask compulsively for directions, the time, the temperature, the hour the *métro* shuts
down. Sometimes all at once. The officers often ask me to re-
peat my questions, while studying me curiously.

"Are you feeling all right, madame?"

I would feel better without them around, but I can't say
that. No more than I can admit to them that this is the third
time today that I've asked for directions from a uniformed officer. The same directions, the same address, and each officer
answers me with the same solicitude, almost reinforcing my
distrust. It's as if they were doing their best to seem pleasant,
since there's no better way to deceive the enemy. And even if
they are what they seem, when I see a uniform, I don't think;
I just succumb to dread, a dog threatened with a stick.

They're there to protect you, repeats a voice in my head, but
I will never be convinced.

Coming home from the Marais neighborhood, where I
had lunch in a little street so calm it seemed like one of my
peaceful memories, I'm pedaling swiftly along. Cars, motor-
cycles, pedestrians go by in a whirl. I like the way I feel on a
bicycle, that sensation of gliding over the asphalt, free and un-
fettered. In a car, I'm closed in. On foot, I'm observed, judged,
spied on. On a bike, I go by so quickly that people have no

time to see my face. I shake off their rules, their codes, I'm simply passing through their world. At the first intersection, however, reality catches up with me, so abruptly I almost get myself killed. Ahead of me, a police van is blocking the road, with a second vehicle parked sideways behind it. My thoughts go crazy; words fall apart in my mind and almost lose their meaning: arrest, police operation, crime, offense . . . Four officers, one of them a woman, have gotten out of the van, and they appear to be arresting someone. Or perhaps they're simply checking something, I don't know. In any case, I don't see the traffic light and I wind up sailing right into them. Forgetting about the hand brakes in my panic, I try to stop by dragging my feet along the pavement; the bicycle hardly slows down at all, swoops through the intersection in a concert of car horns, and crashes into the side of the police van with a dreadful crunching sound.

"Well, well! What happened to you?"

The policewoman is a chubby little blonde with a determined set to her jaw, and I wonder if she often uses that enormous revolver with its hilt sticking halfway up her chest.

One of her colleagues comes to my rescue, helping me regain my balance and handing me my purse, which has fallen to the ground. I observe them both uneasily, trying to detect in their eyes a savage gleam that just isn't there.

"Got to be careful, little lady. Didn't you see that the light was red?"

In reply, I launch into a fawning and complicated mixture of explanations, fake jollity, and flattery. I apologize ten times, and ten times I thank heaven their van was there, or else I would certainly have kept on going, and going, until some car would definitely have run me over. I talk so much I wear them out. They glance meaningfully at one another, and the woman interrupts me.

"Be more careful in the future. Do you know how many cyclists get themselves killed every year in Paris?"

So off I go again, feeling slightly woozy. My enjoyment of the bike ride has turned into a dull anxiety, with a slight edge of relief. As if it were a movie, I replay the scene, which now belongs to my souvenir collection. And I feel shame flood through me, flushing my cheeks. At such moments I loathe my cowardice, that irrepressible impulse to lick people's boots until I can see my reflection in the shine. I remember the childish, confused, pathetic things I said. I go over my excuses and explanations. I would like so much to be insolent and masterful! I would like to be . . . like them.

If my fears were confined to uniforms, I would be the happiest of women. To me, Paris is a festival of aggression, filled with the daily trench warfare of its embittered inhabitants. I am stunned to discover that these free people have spent years sharpening their weapons, growing up into vindictive adults, waving the banners of their petty conflicts.

At cafés, those famous Parisian waiters in their tight-fitting black and white uniforms positively drip with disdain, intim-

idating me almost as much as the cops. I get nervous just thinking about sitting in a café and facing the contempt in their eyes.
I cannot count how many times I've called out to them in a
mousy little voice and been ignored.

"Excuse me!"

The penguin zips by, almost brushing against me, pretending I am invisible.

"Monsieur, please . . ."

"One minute!"

Well, if anyone in Paris has a minute, I do. I have two, ten
even, so many it's pointless to count. Most free people are
painfully dependent on their watches and alarm clocks, an almost physical addiction that makes them cling to each second
as if it were their last. I have all the time in the world. But I hate
this transparency, these eyes that look right through me as if I
were a window onto the void.

After discussing politics with a newspaper vendor and waiting on everyone in the whole world, the penguin reluctantly
hops up to my table.

"What will you have?"

What will I have? It hardly matters. Whatever it is, he will
take my order with a pout of disgust. I must remain calm. There
is a strange unwritten law binding the Parisian café waiter and
his victim into a relationship of domination that reverses the
usual roles: I pay to be ignored, to have someone bark at me.
I pay to be looked down on—if I can get anyone to look my
way at all. Years later, I will learn from foreigners (those free
people who visit us) that this phenomenon is a local one, and

that our surly café waiters are as famously Parisian as the Eiffel Tower.

For now, I dread meeting anyone in a café, where I always arrive half an hour early because I cannot bear being late. Before I even sit down, I steel myself for the coming fray, breathing deeply, gathering my strength. Like a boxer. What weapons do I have against the icy hostility of the native inhabitants? The precepts instilled in me by my Alsatian governess, those sacrosanct good manners drummed into me until they became my second skin.

Stand up for yourself, I'm told. Don't let people walk all over you.

But the rules of my new life are so thoroughly beyond me that I can only swallow my pride and turn the other cheek. Which is what Christians do, at least in theory, to get to Heaven. And if that is how one gets there, well, that is where I'm going, with enough points to sit next to God and sing with the angels. Because for each snarl, I gave back a polite smile; for each check thrown at me, I said thank you; for each nasty comment, I left a tip.

In time, Paris teaches me to fight back. Studying how free people go for the throat over the slightest annoyance, I learn the ropes. Sooner or later, my fear will vanish, and I will return blow for blow. At least I hope so, because no one can live constantly with fear, not even someone who lived tortured by it throughout her youth.

The giant supermarket, that huge amusement park of rampant consumerism, will be my first training ground. As I step out of my car, I know that I will be entering a gladiatorial arena. The supermarketer (that's my word for the mass consumer) has two guiding principles: be quick, and don't let anyone get ahead of you. And even though they're free to go where they want, when they want, how they want, those two things are all free people think about. Their motto is: fast—and faster!

Although I'm fascinated by the sight of grocery shoppers engaged in their chariot race, I don't dare join them at first. The carts are corralled one inside the other and secured by a chain, which opens only when you slip a coin into a small box. Luckily, I watch lots of people do this right in front of me, so I catch on quickly. Everyone's in a hurry, jerking the carts around with a screeching noise that would wake the dead, and a few yards away, other supermarketers are returning their carts, banging them back inside one another with a hellish racket. It's my turn: I pull a coin from my change-purse, gripping it as though it were solid gold (I have been warned so often about thieves!), and timidly claim my chariot for the race.

My cart and I do fairly well, and as my expedition progresses I almost manage to relax. This is child's play, actually, if one steers with a firm hand and watches out for other shoppers popping up on all sides. Concentrating on the race, they don't even notice me, which is enough to make me glad that I came. Being so invisible does unnerve me, of course, but not

nearly as much as conflicts with the natives, with all the inevitable pushing and shouting. For the moment, things are
going so smoothly that I really do feel as if I were on a huge
carousel.

I am gliding nicely into line at the checkout counter when
a cart appears out of nowhere, so jam-packed it looks like a
gypsy caravan, pushed blindly forward by a fat woman in a
flowered dress. Without slowing down, this monstrous mountain of food tries to shove into line right in front of me, clip-
ping my legs painfully in the process. Shocked, I look up at my
adversary, who glares nastily at me, of course. I am angry, but
as usual my stomach knots up and I lower my eyes, which en-
courages the fat woman to continue forcing her way into line.
She bangs my legs again, with the back of her cart, and the pain
is so sharp that I stagger. She gives me another look, but not a
word of apology from those pursed lips. That does it: I explode,
with a miniature Hiroshima that sweeps away (only temporar-
ily, alas) all my doubts, fears, and hesitations. I start to revile
her, to insult her in Arabic so fiercely that I feel as if I were stab-
bing her in the heart. For once, I am not at a loss for words.
They just pour out on their own, an endless flood of acid—so
what if she doesn't understand a thing! The righteous indigna-
tion in my eyes must be something so primal (did I have to wait
for a supermarket to feel hatred at last?) that the fat lady stops
commanding her cart like an Admiral of the Fleet and beats a
stammering retreat.

"This is disgraceful; they should call a security guard," qua-
vers an elderly voice somewhere in the line. Like a bucket of

cold water in my face, the remark brings me back to my senses. And back to the old ghosts that have haunted me ever since I left prison: uniforms, the authorities, breaking the law, interrogations . . . I break off my tirade, but force myself not to give up my hard-won place in line. Is this a victory? I don't know. Acting like a manic shopper is nothing to crow about. But I sense vaguely that Eric will be proud of me—that for the first time, I will not suffer the shame of having turned the other cheek.

5
MODERNITY

I'm back at the Café de Flore, so full of memories, and therefore a place unlike any other, for here I truly can recall that girl I once was, even though I've changed so much since then that I feel I could catch sight of her, sitting there at the next table, without recognizing her. Without recognizing myself. But still, at the Flore I'm almost whole again, complete, a confused combination of my former carefree self and my neuroses of today. The café is stuffy, crowded, and full of cigarette smoke, yet for me it has an aura of Proustian remembrance . . . It is a link between two worlds.

The first time I came back alone to the Flore, my eyes filled with tears. I sat down shyly, ordered a coffee, as in happier days, and sipped at it, savoring the bitterness. I sat there for a long time, quietly, lost in my memories. As always, the air was blue with smoke. The almost deafening racket hardly bothered me, perhaps because it's simply part of the atmosphere—just like the penguins (more unpleasant than ever), all those tourists eager to rub elbows with the ghosts of Sartre and his clique, the neighborhood intellectuals hoping to follow in their elders' footsteps, the well-heeled students with ample spending money, and the walk-in customers who sit stunned by the din.

The room and its décor are much as I remember them, and so I feel that, like me, the Flore has been frozen in time, where it lives in an ageless rhythm, disdaining the rituals of a present I find unfamiliar. And feeling almost moved by such solidarity, I climb the stairs to the ladies' room, sliding my hand along the wooden rail the way one strokes the shoulder of an old friend. When I emerge from the toilet stall, however, the old friend has a laugh at my expense. Because I would like to wash my hands, naturally, and . . . I can't find a hot water faucet, or a cold water faucet, or even some bizarre lever that functions as both of them, like the one in Eric's bathroom.

Don't panic, I tell myself, examining the sink to find where the two faucets have gone.

But they aren't anywhere. A bit embarrassed, I check to see that no one is coming before I start thoroughly examining the premises. The faucets have to be here, it stands to reason. Perhaps these buttons, on the wall? No, those are screws: dead end. There's a kind of ball that sticks out of the wall on the end of a tube: probably the new faucet, which you turn to the left for hot water, and to the right for cold. Putting my theory into practice, I wind up with my hands drenched in liquid soap. There I stand, upset and humiliated, when another woman walks in. I reply to her polite smile with a nod, hiding my soapy hands behind my back. As if to emphasize my ridiculous ineptitude, she washes her hands in the sink, soaping them energetically, and disappears into the toilet stall. Incredulous, I hear the bolt click shut while the water is still dripping. So water comes out for others, but not for me!

I don't have much time; I need to solve this mystery before the woman emerges from the toilet stall. I search again, looking all around the sink: where could she have pushed something? Is there a pedal on the floor? I mean, the water could not have simply *recognized* her, unless they've invented intelligent water, which I seriously doubt. In desperation, I finally kneel to inspect the sink from underneath. Could a button be hidden there? Unless there's a pipe, which I could follow like Ariadne's thread to the magic faucet . . . Caught up in the chase like Howard Carter tracking down Tutankhamen, I am discovered still on my knees by the woman, who emerges from the toilet stall and stares at me in surprise. I stammer, I mumble, I invent some story about a lost earring, and the nice, understanding lady bends down to join me in my search, despite my protestations.

"Oh, don't worry, madame, I'll find it, thank you."

Down at my level, my helper notices that I am wearing two earrings, forcing me to dig myself deeper into my lie by inventing on the spot another pair of earrings, which were in my purse, which fell open accidentally, so one earring fell out, and they are a gift for my sister, which is why I have to find them, in spite of the absurdity of crawling around on all fours in the public bathroom of a café in Saint Germain des Prés. Somewhat convinced by my tall tale, and probably numbed by the details, the woman gets up, gives me a dubious look, and holds her hands under the water spout. Then, miraculously, the water begins to run completely on its own. And kneeling on the floor, as if in prayer, I receive the divine revelation: simply put your hands beneath the spout, and water will gush forth.

The woman has gone, leaving me alone again, head bowed in shame and hands sticky with soap. Gently, I place my hands below the spout: delightfully warm water flows through my fingers. While I was away, the world has learned to do without faucets, sinks have learned to see their customers coming . . . Dear God, have I been asleep for an entire century?

For a long time, when I thought about what it would be like to be free, I wondered about the world outside and whether I would ever be able to adapt to the new ways of thinking, to take part in conversations and figure out the latest slang, the abbreviations, the clues. I didn't know if I would still be able to fit in with people of my generation, or if our shared memories from so long ago would be enough to sustain that connection. Would I still be interested in current events, politics, the movies? I asked myself such questions hundreds of times. But I never, ever, wondered about the evolution of faucets. No one could possibly have imagined that in the time it takes to leave one's youth behind, water would start running all by itself.

And so, the world has decked itself out in a vast array of gadgets, and I cannot help thinking that with all that time the world wasted on soap dispensers, it might have managed to feed the starving, make gasoline from carrots, or repair the ozone layer. I don't know whether to be fascinated or distressed, but one thing is clear: I am a child, an infant in an adult body, and if this disorientation keeps up, I will have to learn how to use a fork all over again.

The welfare state knows how to rub us the right way. I am told that from now on, my every illness, large or small, will be taken care of by the National Health Service, a sort of administrative monster that will reimburse us—if we just sacrifice enough time and red tape to its demands—for even the nose drops we use between two sneezes.

You should go sign up with them, people tell me, without daring to mention that my years in prison have certainly not improved my health. And I'm not alone in this: all of us, my entire family, bear on our bodies the consequences of those terrible years. Mimi (Myriam) has epileptic seizures, Maria had bladder cancer, Raouf goes from bouts of pneumonia to infections, whereas the youngest, Abdellatif, is sick to his very soul.

Registering with the National Health Service will be no trouble at all, supposedly, simply a few formalities. Eric helps me get my documents together: papers vouching for my birth, vaccinations, educational degrees, place of domicile, payment of utility bills, and so on. They all end up in a briefcase, a leather satchel containing everything I am, translated into codes and numbers.

Hidden down a dead-end street and behind an unpronounceable acronym, the National Health Service building resembles a train station lobby. I am still not used to losing myself in a crowd, and am immediately repelled by the noise, the waiting, the smell of concentrated humanity, and the stress hovering everywhere like a threat. What had I expected? A small, spotless office; a few green plants; a warmly smiling receptionist; my name in block letters on an appointment list . . .

Instead, there are individual plexiglass aquariums where harried employees see people for a few brief moments. Sitting on chairs as uncomfortable as a guilty conscience, the customers—is that what they're called, like people in a supermarket?—argue, twisting around in their seats, gesturing vividly and knocking over their discount-store shopping bags. But before they reach the aquariums, they enter a room, an immense room with orange couches where hordes of free people freely indulge in their favorite sport: waiting.

Standing there holding my precious briefcase, I feel watched, and my cheeks flush crimson. Why am I the only person not sitting down? Now I can't bear their eyes on me, and my legs start to feel paralyzed: the numbness creeps up my spine as if I were changing into a pillar of salt, doomed to decorate forever the waiting room of the National Health Service, plunked on a pedestal labeled: Dedicated to the Memory of Stateless People Everywhere.

When a little bell rings, thirty pairs of eyes look up instantly at a digital sign hanging over the aquariums: 164. Someone gets up, goes over to an aquarium.

164 . . . Perplexed, I wonder how to interpret this number. Was his appointment for a set time? Unlikely, since it's eleven in the morning, and no matter how you fiddle with 164, you'll never get anything but 16:04 (4:04 in the afternoon, European style) or perhaps 16:40, which don't really fit. That leaves assigned numbers, issued to all the customers of this venerable institution. Perhaps they're all numbered, ink-stamped like prisoners; I was told that the National Health Service number I would receive would be my passport for all my professional undertakings. My heart sinks: what if everyone here has a number, and I don't?

At that moment, a customer leaves a cubicle and heads for the exit. The digital number switches promptly to 165, with the same little ding. A youth in a jogging suit gets up and glances defiantly at me as he passes by, his walkman blaring. Now I understand . . . He is customer 165 this morning, today, this week, whatever. But how does he know? Maybe they are all used to keeping track among themselves, and that's why they were all watching me suspiciously. By just standing there, I was probably throwing them off their count. Disconcerted, I sit down, determined to let them all go ahead of me.

And so the hours pass, long hours during which some people leave, others arrive, and numbers parade across the digital screen without anyone paying the slightest attention to me. Standing up, I existed; sitting, I am simply furniture. 170, 180, 190. I watch everyone come and go in this endlessly busy place. When I can't take any more of that, I venture over to the aquariums, where, trying to hide my nervousness and hoping that someone will notice me, I wait. For a long time. I wait while a "customer" spends fifteen minutes detailing the terrible dilemma of some mail he did not receive, which seems to be preventing him from receiving his rightful due. No, he has not sent in a claim. No, he did not keep a copy of that medical record.

No, he does not feel like waiting for the welfare state to finally find his file. And here comes the shouting: "I pay taxes, madame, I have been paying my share for twenty years, and given the generous salary you earn, it's a disgrace that I can't get a simple reimbursement!"

As cold as an Arctic winter, the West Indian employee blames the problem on the post office, the sorting department, the repayment bureau, some kind of insurance company, and other organizations with acronyms that sound to me like Swahili. The guy does not back down and takes on the government, the Right, the Left, various dead French presidents, plus the authorities' nefarious plot against his eyeglasses prescription.

"And I'm not talking about the Arabs," he rages, "who've never worked a day in their lives and have no problem getting reimbursed, not them. Me, I know those people: give 'em a hand, and they'll take your whole arm. Oh, they really know how to work the system: mother, daughter, sons, uncles, grand-parents—they don't even have their papers in order and you reimburse them for every last cent. And who pays for it? I ask you!"

This particular Arab waits obediently in the doorway until the swindled customer stomps out with all the dignity of his injured pride, but not before threatening the employee with hellfire and, even worse, a registered letter. I feel sorry for the woman, imagining myself in her place, roundly insulted by a lout on the wrong end of a dispute. And that's not the half of it: how does she manage, this free woman, to spend eight hours a day in a neon-lit, glass-paneled broom closet, where everyone comes to dump all the ills of society on her? A sudden rush of sympathy almost dispels my fears, and with spontaneous warmth I bestow upon her a friendly "Good morning, madame" that barely gets me a quick glance.

"One-ninety?"

Instant paralysis.

"Excuse me?"

She waves impatiently at the digital screen overhead.

"One-ninety. It's right in front of you."

Drawing on my impeccable education, I launch into a flowery yet respectful speech, explaining that no, I am not 190, or indeed any other number, that I have come simply to register with the National Health Service, that no one warned me that I needed a number, and that I would be ever so grateful if she were to inform me how I might obtain my very own number, like a cow at a slaughterhouse.

Without batting an eye, the West Indian woman looks up at me in irritation.

"I don't understand. Didn't you take a number?"

"No, madame."

"Take a number," she says, pointing to a machine over at the entrance, which I had mistaken for a fire extinguisher. "And wait until you're called."

For a moment I wonder if I will spend the night—and even longer—in this antechamber of the Absurd. So: that strange red snail attached to the wall by the entrance is not a fire extinguisher, but a ticket dispenser. And yes, one is sticking out, number 229. My number. But I still have to convince the snail to let go of the ticket. And I don't see any button to make it pop out, or any lever to turn what is probably an endless roll of tickets. Timidly, I grasp the end of the ticket between my thumb and index finger, but the thing resists, hangs back. I run a cautious finger over the snail's shell, hoping to find a hidden mechanism, but it's depressingly smooth. Should I follow the example of the magic water faucet, wiggling my hand beneath an invisible electric eye to make the ticket drop into my palm? That doesn't work. I even try taking a few steps backward and forward, in case the detector isn't under the machine, but somewhere around it. Now I think I'm Jules Verne or Leonardo da Vinci, imagining a future that dispenses tickets as soon as a customer walks through the door.

My ritual dance before the snail has not, alas, gone unobserved. What can I do now? Go back to the aquarium and admit my ignorance? I'd rather die . . . That's when a new arrival enters, steps in front of me as if I did not exist, and after giving my ticket—229—a sharp tug, walks off with it. Aha! This fire extinguisher resembling a flying saucer is just a simple box with a ticket roll inside, like those large toilet paper dispensers in public bathrooms. And the bit of paper in front of me is number 230, the wretched ticket for which I have just wasted half a day of my life.

The underside of the modern world is beneath our feet. Kilometers of tunnels, sewers, galleries, métro entrances, and underground parking garages going down two, three, four, even six levels beneath the surface. I can't help thinking about them whenever I stroll along the overcrowded boulevards of the capital. They form an entire world a few yards below us, a realm of shadows untouched by the summer sunshine above. It didn't take me long to notice that free people don't like to go underground, even if they spend a good part of their lives there. They're a little like children who demand a night-light, a last defense against the darkness, and subterranean spaces embody this fear and distress. The métro, cellars, underground garages: all so many places where the specter of aggression— that supreme obsession of every self-respecting city-dweller— hovers threateningly. Yet Paris is a relatively safe city, and even if it were dangerous, why would the underground areas be less secure than the alleyways of the old market neighborhood of Les Halles, where young derelicts sniff glue in doorways?

In short, I, who am afraid of everyone and everything, have not the slightest objection to going underground—indeed, I even find it quite peaceful there, as if, far from the light and bustle of the world aboveground, I were finally able to withdraw within myself. Up in the world of light, I am onstage, where, dying of stage fright, I must watch my every move. Below ground, I can allow myself to reflect, to read, lulled by the dull hum of the métro.

I have never understood why I feel threatened by crowds outdoors, whereas they never bother me in the métro—except during rush hours, when free people are packed together like sardines, and the smell of my neighbor's breath can be sickening. Otherwise, I am—at last—indifferent to my fellow passengers. Do I exist for them? I don't know, and for once, I don't care. Give me even the corner of a seat to myself, and I am off, embarked on a voyage I wish would never end, to the reassuring cadence of the cars rattling along the rails. It's there, underground, that I escape daily life and lose myself in a book. Now and then I look up, not so much to watch the stations slip by as to stare out into the darkness of the tunnels. At the Réaumur-Sébastopol station, I noticed that colonies of diminutive mice lived in the metal frames of the seats on which waiting travelers read their newspapers. No one ever turned around to observe the tiny muzzles sticking out of the small holes, because people have only one preoccupation: to return to the light as soon as possible. I, on the other hand, have poked a few bits of cookie into the holes, and felt them snatched at from the other side. Although much is said about the rats that live underground, I personally have seen only those small mice, curiously adept at surviving in a concrete universe.

There are also people in that universe, especially when summer gives way to snow and ice. I have been told that the métro seats are now spaced a good yard apart not, as I had thought, to allow me to read in peace, but to keep these underground people from lying down on them. Free people do not like the sight of someone else's misfortune. And unlike the mice, the "homeless" cannot duck inside holes to shield themselves from the cold and other people's eyes.

I am even fonder, perhaps, of parking garages, because they are always deserted. You might notice some figures hugging the walls, desperately looking for their cars, but for the most part, as far as the eye can see stretch endless lines of empty vehicles bathed in an impersonal neon glare. As I go by, I make up a story for each car: a driver, a family, abstract people who will never frighten me because I have created them, and they belong to me. For many years I used to invent characters and stories to open new horizons in my closed universe. I kept my family in suspense with episodes of a story that lasted our whole time in prison and that lived, evolved, grew old along with us. It was the imaginary tale of imaginary people developing within a universe that I pretended was real. A caged Scheherazade, I invented, night after night, a story that took place in nineteenth-century Russia. In "The Black

Snowflakes," I described, with an accuracy all the more mysterious for never having set foot in Russia, the palace of St. Petersburg, Cossack charges, sleigh rides on the frozen Volga. I had imagination to spare! Outside was the furnace of the Moroccan night, but in our hearts were imaginary snowdrifts. Every one of us dreamed, and Raouf whistled to alert me when my voice grew too low for him to hear.

Inevitably, the main characters of those stories became so familiar that I feel as if I've lived by their side. That is how one becomes a writer, or a schizophrenic. There is something of that narrative in the serried ranks of cars that crowd the parking garages beneath Paris, for the cars are empty boxes echoing with stories for anyone who wants to listen. It is a world that is made for me, where no one will judge you because there is no one there.

6

WEALTH

For as far back as I remember, my fortune fit into my purse. True, like most people I had a savings account—in my case, one suitable for a girl of good family—and I led the carefree life of those who have never lacked for anything. But money remained a concrete thing, an oh-so-palpable concept that jingled in my pockets. In the 1970s, a checkbook was anything but a toy, and it was with a certain solemnity that I filled out and signed the slips of paper that would dip into my account for the benefit of the Left Bank couturiers.

In the world of free people, money itself has been fundamentally transformed. After remaining intact and unchanging for centuries, it was suddenly revamped while I was away in prison. Does everything have to elude me, as if to punish me for having been gone so long? Paper money still exists, of course, as do coins, which the French call white or yellow, depending on their value and the color of the metal. Old folks can cling to those, as well as to the good old check, which was invented at least two hundred years ago. When I moved to Paris, before the euro replaced the "new" franc, there were even people who still calculated in *old* francs, but the truth is, modern money has an even more radical new face. It has become abstract, volatile, and people put it into play as if the coins were chips in a casino.

My fortune now resides in a small piece of plastic, which is casually handed over to the waiter without even a pause in the conversation. Not three months ago, I was astounded by the magic of the credit card machine, swearing at the same time that I would never use such rarefied methods myself. Pay with thin air? No way. I have to see my money, touch it, count the bills I have left, figure out in my head how much change I should receive and the tip I should leave. The idea of credit worries me, cuts me off from reality. And yet . . . Anxious not to see me live in the past like those old folks who still have not adopted checks, let alone bank cards, Eric got me a Blue Card (called a debit card in the States), nice and shiny, which bears my name in gold letters alongside a hologram I never tire of admiring. With this golden passkey, he said, I would never have a problem: I could use it almost everywhere to buy things, and where it wasn't accepted, automated teller machines would take over, changing the plastic to cash, a veritable alchemist's dream. All around me I see free people collecting these cards with obvious pride, while wallets and billfolds have followed the fashion, adding a flap to hold up to ten credit cards—or simply turning completely into credit card cases. There was a time when a sure sign of success was being able to flash a thick roll of bills, but today the ultimate is to carry around a card case sporting all the colors of the rainbow. There are cards for every taste and budget, but the main thing is to acquire enough so you can feel you exist. Because the world that I came back to can recognize and acknowledge you only through a gigantic network of credit.

At first my Blue Card stayed put in the bottom of my purse, which only increased my fears that it might be stolen. Of course, this object invented to make life easier actually made mine worse, adding one more worry to an already flourishing collection.

"What if someone steals it?"

"No one will steal it," Eric assured me. "Worst case, you make a phone call to block the card."

A phone call? In my wildest dreams I would never think of disturbing a banker at his work to admit that I have foolishly lost my Blue Card. I would definitely get into trouble: he would criticize me, scorn me, fine me, perhaps. I carried that burdensome card like a kid wearing her house key around her neck: with so many things depending on such a small item, even the thought of losing it can ruin the whole day.

Luckily (so to speak), unlike the house-key necklace, a credit card is protected by a code, four magic numbers without which it isn't much use. I was strongly urged to learn my code by heart, but—what if I forgot it? Three botched attempts to use it and the card is automatically frozen (don't ask me how) and won't work. What happens then? I don't even want to know. The bank is probably alerted, perhaps the police are called, since a code-less card means a stolen card. And that is how four numbers came to invade my life, settling in everywhere, clamoring for my attention as often as possible. I wrote them on the back of my little notebook, on a folded piece of paper tucked into my wallet, on a pad of paper at home, on a Post-it stuck to the refrigerator, and even, with a felt-tip pen, on the inside of my wrist. Result: I remember those numbers as if they were my date of birth, but who knows, I just might happen to forget them one time; it's better to be safe.

"It really isn't a good idea to walk around with the code in your purse," someone finally told me. "If somebody steals it, he's got everything he needs to clean out your account!"

For a long time, I avoided cash machines. I could handle using a credit card when running errands, and I even became used to shopping for food and clothes with a slip of plastic, but withdrawing cash from a machine right out on the street was something else entirely. Every time I got ready to use one of those machines, I had the horrible feeling that I was setting myself up to be mugged, and I would trudge off in discouragement, like a budding bank robber haunting the entrance of a bank he doesn't dare enter. CIC, CCF, Crédit Lyonnais, Société Générale, Banque Nationale de Paris—so many machines spread throughout Paris, tempting you to withdraw money. They even have illuminated signs showing a hand slipping a card into a slot, the perfect invitation to a spending spree. These signs are part of the city landscape, just like the new bus shelters plastered with advertisements, which have largely replaced the familiar Morris columns that used to carry film and theater ads.

But fate always tracks you down, and I wound up one fine morning on line in front of a CIC machine somewhere around the Gare de Lyon train station. I had no choice: I needed money and didn't have time to go home or to the bank. A blue and red cash machine just down the street looked at me invitingly, and I gave in, but not without a struggle: I walked by the machine a few times, gave it some suspicious looks, then sidled up to it, hoping we could become friends. I felt that unmistakable, gut-wrenching rush of dread and anguish, a mix of emotions that doesn't really have a name. And if I had to choose one, I'd call it . . . free-world syndrome.

And now I'm on line in front of the machine, while my brain is panicking with questions. Will I understand how the machine works? Don't count on it. Will it recognize my card, the way the water spout at the Café de Flore can see people's hands? Won't the machine ask me for some other code, a bank account number, an endorsement from my banker, my Social Security number? The worst thing is, the line is growing behind me: a woman and a man in work clothes are grumbling about waiting their turn, already irritated because the person at the machine isn't moving fast enough, which in this progressive day and age has become a mortal sin. The workman sighs noisily. The woman checks her watch. The thought of fleeing crosses my mind, but I know that things would be the same anywhere else. It's noon, Paris is swarming with people, and in this busy neighborhood I will not find a cash machine off in some lonely corner where I might learn how to use it in private.

It's my turn. And someone else has just lined up behind me. I can't take it—I turn around to the woman in back of me.

"Would you like to go ahead of me, madame?"

"No, thank you. You were here first."

I mumble my thanks (for what?) and turn back to the monster. With delicious irony, a colorful screen bids me "Welcome," along with "Please enter your card." In case I am too dumb to understand, a small drawing of my hand, my card, the slot, and even the number pad in front of me drives the point home.

Slowly, glancing to either side, I take out my card, petrified at the idea that just anyone could pounce on me and race off with my entire fortune. I turn around suddenly: maybe *that's* why the woman behind me declined to take my turn . . . But she hasn't budged, and is busy rummaging in her purse while the construction worker waits impatiently behind her. So I dip my card into the slot, but the instant I feel a tug on it—because our cash machines ingest the card whole, then spit it out again—I hold it tighter, refusing to let go. The creepy machine wants to swallow it, and *what if it won't give it back?* What if my card vanishes forever, without a trace? Even worse, what if it gets coughed up again a few hours later, when anyone at all could grab it and clean out masses of boutiques at my expense? I struggle for a few seconds with the hungry machine, then snatch back the card. Taking a deep breath, I compose myself. The machine did not have time to identify me: the screen still says "Welcome," and the worker behind me heaves another sigh of frustration. I guess I really must let my most precious possession disappear into the invisible bowels of this machine. I bring my card once again up to the mouth of the CIC monster, which immediately chomps on it. Unwillingly, like a lover forced to let go of the beloved's hand on a train platform, I release my card so that it can live its own life. I hear a mechanical grinding, a few hisses, and the screen changes color. "Please enter your personal code." Enter my secret code, here, in the middle of the street? I turn around again.

"You plan on spending the night here?" growls the workman, only too happy to tell me what he thinks.

I stammer some feeble explanation, then wriggle around, trying to make my back broader, and feverishly tap in my four numbers. The screen snaps back, "Incorrect code, try again." I feel an instant chill down my spine, especially since the numbers I type turn into asterisks, leaving me no way to tell if I have made a mistake. The horror mounts: the screen announces, "Second attempt." My second try, already? I know that after the third one, I will be lost, and my card with me.

Going through the motions, I dig into my wallet to check the numbers, which have not changed, of course, because numbers do not just change from one minute to the next. The machine likes my second try, fortunately, and shows me a new screen: 200, 400, 600, 800, Other. How do I get 200 francs? I try typing in 200, to no avail. Desperate, I push one of the arrows surrounding the screen, which leads to a sinister "Please be patient." "We are contacting your bank," announces the machine, and my heart stops. Why are they doing that? I haven't done anything wrong . . .

"Please retrieve your card." I snatch up my card and stuff it into my pocket, relieved that the worst is over. After more metallic noise, a flap opens and bills so new they look fake slide toward me. Two hundred francs—once, twice, three times. Six hundred francs! I stare in alarm at the bills, counting and recounting them. The machine has made a mistake, I am sure of it, and has given me someone else's money. I almost feel like giving the money to the people waiting on line; perhaps it's theirs.

At the first telephone booth I see, I call Eric to tell him what has happened and beg him to call the bank, to let them know that a couple of two-hundred-franc bills from someone else's account are floating around the city. I am prepared to give them back, immediately if necessary, if this damned cash machine would just work backward and inhale the money the way it does bank cards.

"Don't worry about it," the man of my life reassures me. "You must have pushed the wrong button, that's all."

It seems that automatic teller machines never make mistakes, just as the sink in the *Café de Flore* never refuses to turn on the water for a waiting pair of hands. Perhaps I did push the wrong button, choose the wrong arrow, or the amounts were in the wrong order, but whatever the case, these money-spitting monsters, these bank tellers that never sleep, don't give you someone else's money. Ever. Vaguely relieved, I will still spend the next two weeks with that pit-of-the-stomach feeling that I have broken some law, until my bank statement arrives to confirm a withdrawal of six hundred francs on the date when I went up against the dreaded Machine from Hell.

And yet, I cannot bring myself to accept the principle of credit. My education, my values, the long absence that cut me off from the ways of the world, all tend to make me reject this general eagerness to spend money that does not exist. I was a helpless prisoner for too long to willingly chain myself to the anxieties of life on the installment plan. People who live in freedom are tempted by so many enticing things, their dreams are stocked with so many treasures, that they're ready to commit them-selves for ten, twenty years, a sentence without appeal, just for a new car. What's so special about a car that makes them bor-row money at so-called preferential rates? Leather seats, air con-ditioning, a nice color, fancy hubcaps? Big deal. If it were up to me, Eric and I would live for twenty years with the same pre-historic Peugeot, and all the money we'd save by not buying a shiny new Mercedes would go into a savings account for a rainy day. My long exploration of the ghostly existence of prison life has few advantages, but at least I've learned that my needs will never be the same as those of free people. Like them, I was once young and carefree, a blithe victim of fashion and the consumer society. Today I know things that others sometimes take a lifetime to understand. Unlike most of humanity, I am not driven by an insatiable hunger.

I have to say that since my return to the outside world, I have been dismayed by the way advertising has taken over our lives. Years ago, consumerism was already flexing its muscles, but unless prison has tampered with my memories, we endured nothing like the maelstrom of modern advertising. The walls of Paris are papered with posters touting yogurts, clothing, perfumes. Television is a fireworks display of so many ads that my mind reels: they come at us before, after, even during the programs. Between the news and the weather, up pops a supermarket or an optician. Different shows are brought to you by various "sponsors." In magazines, half the pages try to tantalize free people with the delights of things they do not possess. Lagoons with turquoise water glitter on the walls of the métro, stamped "Special offer!" to jump-start vacation dreams. Dirt-cheap flights to the ends of the earth, office computers, stereo systems, all-terrain bikes, diamonds to say "I love you," and foie gras in glass jars—there's something for everyone, for all ages. Even the elderly (now called "seniors," because we no longer call things by their names), who should have reached the age of wisdom, are lured into stores by ergonomic recliner chairs in which they can sit alone and stupefied in front of the TV, or by garden furniture they will carefully arrange beside their flowerbeds, awaiting the day when their children, who stopped coming long ago, might decide to visit. Even worse, the elderly are urged to buy their own funerals, life insurance, and cemetery plots, so that they won't be any bother when the time comes for them to stop consuming.

7
POVERTY

Albert is my friend. Yet he is no one's friend, for everyone goes by him without seeing him. He is part of the landscape, like the street signs or the trash can on the corner. Nowadays, instead of "tramp" (the term was banished while I was away), people say "homeless person," or even "WFD" ("without fixed domicile"), to save time. Come nightfall, however, Albert does have a home, an almost fixed one, in a nook below the display window of a shoe store. Beneath pairs of fifteen-hundred-franc pumps, he sets up his little nest: a sleeping bag, a rolled-up jacket for a pillow, and a McDonald's cup sitting on the sidewalk, in case someone feels like getting rid of those small coins that make suit pockets bulge so unattractively. Albert sleeps there every evening, except on the harshest winter nights, when white buses pick up the homeless so that they will not freeze to death. Once or twice, he has had to decamp, chased away by riverside residents bothered by the smell, or by the shop owner returning to do his accounts. And one summer night, a gang of youths beat him up for free, just for fun.

Albert is my friend, and I mean that. If I merely contributed to his beggar's bowl now and again, my only motive would be pity. But that's not it at all. Unlike many others in this free world, I feel fine around the homeless, even better, in fact, than I do around people with fixed domiciles, who inevitably make me nervous. The thing is, the homeless do not cheat. They are wholly themselves, completely up front, and I recognize myself in their naive and desperate way of perceiving the world. How many times have I heard Albert and his fellow bums ramble on about this and that, about life and poverty? I don't know, but I feel as if I have spent more time with them than with my friends. The homeless turn a deaf ear, as I do, to the siren call of advertising, because how can people fantasize about the new Seat—comes equipped with four airbags!—when they go to bed hungry?

Albert is forty years old, and his erratic life has led him to the foot of my apartment building. Now and then he tells me about his years of wandering; on other occasions, he opens his heart, talking about how his days can drag on, about times when the cup just won't fill up. He is curious about me, too, without any sham politeness, without any of the empty formulas employed by people who try so hard to show their interest in you that they forget to listen to you. Begging embarrasses me, and I really do not like slipping money to Albert. Strangely enough, although it is good form to assume that beggars must feel ashamed, I am the one made uneasy by an outstretched hand. Every so often I manage to give him some money without it looking like charity. Or I make sure I have a little something for him, a bit of food, a bottle, a newspaper.

Whether they are eating, drinking, smoking, or doing drugs, the Alberts of this world live on the margins of human society, tossed out on the sidewalks like garbage bags, their only goal to survive. Well, I know what it's like, that fierce struggle to make it to tomorrow, without really knowing why. The survival instinct, hope, force of habit—I have no idea what pushes desperate souls to hang on until the bitter end.

Every day, my money vanishes by the handful in the métro, sucked up by all the needy in that underworld: the homeless, beggars, street musicians, newspaper sellers, candy hawkers—shuffling from car to car, endlessly reciting the same come-ons, they pass furtively through the world of free men and women, who look down at the floor at their approach. A child to feed, a roof for the night, enough to get a hot meal, a few coins toward the rent . . . Is there some truth to any of it? Yes or no, it doesn't matter: I instinctively feel their distress. They are always there, cruising the cars, holding out their hands in the subway passages or outside in the sunshine, on the stairs. Their litanies have become so much a part of the city's white noise that passengers barely notice them anymore, beyond frowning with bored exasperation and concentrating on their reading. In this free society, people exercise the freedom to ignore the poverty around them: they find it only natural to close themselves off. When I see them buried in their magazines or studying their shoes, I sometimes wonder about that shell they shut so easily. Are they trying to forget that one day they might be joining Albert in his gray little world? Perhaps they are only calculating the contents of their wallets: if they run out of small coins, they might have to break a bill when they feel like having some coffee.

As for me, I pay, without rhyme or reason (without reason, according to my friends, who assure me that a veritable Mafia of beggary runs riot in Paris). The few coins I give are not much, and do not much satisfy me, although most people feel that a few francs tossed into a cap will buy a clear conscience.

Thanks to Albert and his friends, I decide to make myself useful, to forget my own neuroses by helping those who sleep out in the rain. So, in all innocence, I join a voluntary organization with the Parisian Homeless Outreach Program, because that might be where we all ought to find our personal equilibrium, a better way to stop contemplating our own navels than paying a thousand francs an hour to mumble introspective monologues. Newly determined, I blithely set out to assist society's rejects. But the street has a way of trashing grand ideas. In one night, I see a side of Paris I never knew existed, an appalling world of filth and vermin. Through the one-way windows of the EMS bus, the lights of the city twinkle like stars, and I just want to go home. My fine resolutions, newfound strength, magic do-gooder's wand—all gone up in smoke: I huddle in my seat, aghast at so much sadness. Feeling too shaken to go on, I give up after one pathetic night of service, leaving with enough raw material for years of nightmares.

"Don't feel bad," the coordinator consoles me. "Most people can't take it."

It's hard for me to tell her that I feel terrible, ashamed of my cowardice. The worst is that I had loudly informed everyone about my new humanitarian adventure, even going so far as to lecture others for ignoring the plight of the homeless. And a single night taught me that I did not have the backbone to face any more distress beyond my own. For a few days, I studiously avoided the shoe store window and the face of my friend Albert.

At the Gare Saint Lazare, I see a different side of human misery in the person of an old woman walking slowly along a train platform. She is lugging a heavy suitcase, a tote-bag, and a cane, and there is clearly no one waiting to meet her. Her shoes are worn-out, her suitcase battered, her clothing gray and threadbare, like the years that weigh her down. I watch her struggle along, a poor, stooped figure, amid the throng pouring from the train. Is she returning from a trip, or does she live, like so many others, in some dark corner of the station? I have no way of knowing. Travelers hurrying past sometimes get caught on her cane and almost bump into her. Seventy years on this earth to end up alone, clinging to some luggage . . .

The world I come from is far from perfect, but it taught me respect for my elders, for the value of wisdom, traditions, and family. I remember gatherings where venerable old women sat in state, telling enthralling stories far into the night. In the East, no one wants to die before reaching an honorable old age.

People who are free are also free to look away, and their willingness to do so never fails to astound me. It also explains the unbelievable newspaper headlines: a girl raped in a subway car full of passengers, a man attacked in broad daylight on the Champs-Elysées, ten-year-olds victimized during recess by extortionist classmates. In the twenty years while I was gone, I think the cult of the individual went mad.

This tendency to look the other way leaps out at me as I watch that old woman advance alone toward her fate, ignored by her fellow-passengers. She could collapse and die on this platform without anyone coming to her aid. At best, somebody might call the emergency service or the station manager. But in this world of freedom, what I see in people's eyes is embarrassment. It is not really indifference that makes them look away, or talk louder, or hurry up—it's shame. Dear God, how much simpler it would be to take her arm, smile at her, help carry her bags! While Paris has been filling up with magic water faucets, communication has become so difficult that it is now easier to swallow one's discomfort than to extend a helping hand.

No one knows that better than Albert, who watches people step over his cup as if it weren't there, and who falls asleep curled up like a dog, with an empty heart and belly.

FREEDOM

"You'll never be able to rescue all the strays," people tell me, whenever I upset myself over the human misery on every street corner. I know that. I have enough troubles of my own without worrying about those of others, but distress calls out to me: it's stronger than I am, and I just can't look the other way.

8
AT THE TABLE

I come from a world where every crumb counts. For years, I collected and saved so many of them that if they were laid out in a line, it would lead all the way back to Morocco. In the fairy tales of my childhood, Tom Thumb used pebbles instead of bread crumbs to leave a trail back to his house, but I would have given anything never to be found again, so that I could leave behind the house that an ogre with a crown had filled with suffering.

Crumbs do not count in the world of freedom, and neither does the bread they come from. It is sliced up in haste, tossed into a basket, and set out to decorate a table. At best, it sops up some sauce or is nibbled on, dipped in mustard, before the "real" food arrives. Bread is there for amusement, because sitting at a table is almost a game, one with its codes, rules, ritual courtesies, and its decorative bread baskets that will be emptied into huge garbage cans when the meal is over, the way one empties an ashtray.

I had so much trouble getting used to stores and their kilometers of shelves, their hundred varieties of sausage by the meter, that the special realm of restaurants felt like a fresh ordeal. And an inescapable one, since the free world pivots around the table: everything connects to it—friendship, love, business, family. Eating is a passport for everything and nothing.

"Whenever you're ready, dear, we'll have lunch."

We'll have lunch . . . Which means that we will go to a restaurant crowded with people who came to talk, conduct business, begin a seduction or break off an affair, stare into one another's eyes, sign a contract, or hold hands. Who cares about one's plate? The gourmands, the gourmets do (the label does not matter): those who take pride in paying through the nose for a "little farandole" of deluxe crumbs arranged in arabesques, so that it is not always possible to know what is food and what is just garnish. Here, a carrot cut into a rose by a true artist; there, a dribble of sauce in a question mark, so thin it seems drawn by a master Japanese calligrapher. What about the tiny vegetables arranged in a star, or the slender sage leaf that crowns the ensemble? Impossible to say. If in doubt, I would push the whole thing to the side of the plate. Because *la grande cuisine* leaves me even more perplexed than does cooking in general.

Grand cuisine showcases food, but silliness as well. And while the food at the corner bistro is only a pretext for chatting, in the finer restaurants it allows the wealthy to indulge in a veritable ceremony of prestige. I watch them strike poses, delving into the menu with the panache of a poet. "Nibbles of wild mantis, lobster jus à la green asparagus, and tiny salt-crusted new potatoes from Zealand." For a translation, I must wait until a maître d' with a broomstick down his back tip-toes over to my table so reverently that he might almost be carrying the Son of God: "Three little mantis-crab fritters with a dab of sauce and some salty Dutch potatoes."

One mouthful and the crab is gone, along with the three hundred francs it cost. Entrée, cheese, dessert, coffee, and liqueur will follow to justify an astronomical bill of a thousand francs per person, maybe more (I can see the numbers only from the corner of my eye; women receive an aseptic menu, without prices). A thousand francs? Enough to feed a legion of those homeless people sleeping just a few doors away, who would be happy just to have some food, never mind the fancy names.

But the most incredible part is the meal before the meal. While we were perusing the menu (which admittedly took as long to read, given the endless descriptions of each dish, as the Bible), the waiter brought us a platter of *amuse-bouches,* a selection of palate pleasers including petits fours, baby quiches, and mini-mouthfuls. Everything imaginable was there and then some, in minute versions, like a gala banquet in a dollhouse: fish, meat, savory tartlets, creams, mousses, sauces, vegetables, shrimp, puff pastry, pizza tidbits. All on a silver platter.

❧

For twenty years, in a prison where rats and mice alone could eat their fill, I ate to survive. Which marks you, obviously. So that you can no longer eat for amusement, or while chatting about the state of the world. You cannot eat frivolously, without anxiety. While people in the world of freedom were bickering over what to have with their filet mignon ("More gratin dauphinois? I just had some, the day before yesterday!"), our family was living on one liter of oil a month, one candle per person, a dozen eggs every two weeks. Twelve rotten eggs, which for a long time were a culinary treasure to me.

To anyone stocking up on cartons of organic eggs or ordering an omelet on the terrace of the Café Flore, "rotten" is a relative term. To me, an egg is not spoiled when it has passed its sell-by date, but when the shell (which the free world thinks of as white or brown) has acquired a greenish tinge. For twenty years, that is what our eggs were like, and my youngest brother, who grew up in prison, did not see a fresh egg until we were released. Our eggs had no whites and no yellows: they were black as ink, a reminder of the hole where we'd been left to rot.

Acting as chef for the feast that highlighted our usual fare twice a month, I would break the green eggs into a tin bowl to let the black liquid settle. During the night, the unspeakable stench would improve just enough for us to eat this nightmarish slop, which free people would not feed to their dogs for fear of poisoning them. By dipping a crust of stale bread into the egg (now mixed with a pinch of powdered milk, a sprinkle of sugar, and a soupspoon of oil), I would make a kind of "pancake" we adored. And the smell of frying that wafted through the cells was a treat, worth more to us than all the mantis crabs that ever lived.

As for the bread, we used to spend a lot of time sitting in a circle trying to brush the mold and the mouse turds off it. We had to keep our supply hidden under a flat stone, in our "breadbox": a hole in the dirt where rats would get in to chew and pee on it. Like the eggs, our bread was black. I suppose that where food is concerned, light colors are the hallmark of freedom. Every morsel, every crust was precious, because it swelled our pantry. That was our supermarket, our plain cooking and haute cuisine, depending on the ingredients we could procure. Even today, so long afterward, I bridle at the sight of people engrossed in conversation who pick idly at their bread and drop little wads of it in the ashtray. How many diners, once they have rolled all the soft part into tiny balls, reach automatically for a second piece to reduce that one as well to crumbs, and all without eating a single bite of it?

So long as I keep comparing my present life to my past, I'll see everyone and everything with frightened eyes. But my past takes up most of my life. And my life right now is so hard for me to understand . . . How much longer will this way of looking at the world keep me from moving on? In prison, I longed obsessively for freedom. Now that I'm free, I seek escape . . .

And hope.

The woman interviewing me is forty, perhaps a little older. She has insisted that we sit in a restaurant to discuss the fact that for twenty years, I was starving.

"Let's do lunch, it'll be nicer," she had told me on the phone, this woman whom I have never met.

Nice is not quite the word, for as soon as she arrives, the journalist frowns at the menu, complains that the pizza with tuna does not come with anchovies, hopes she will be able to have onions instead of peppers, because she does not like peppers, at least cooked peppers, whereas raw or marinated ones she can deal with, and she wants to know if I like them, cooked peppers—perhaps she will put that in her article. I begin to understand why I never read her newspaper.

Next come a good ten minutes of negotiations with the waitress, who is not sure about the peppers, she will have to check with the chef.

"The last time, the egg wasn't cooked enough," adds the journalist. "That's the kind of thing that can just spoil your whole day."

"Don't worry, I'll tell the kitchen."

"Well, I should hope so!"

Now she turns to me, repeats that an uncooked egg sits too heavily on the stomach, don't I agree, but I pass, so she switches to another topic, but not before fussing over the absence of an ashtray, and the inexcusable fact that the Perrier is lukewarm. Ice cubes? No, they make it taste funny.

"Let's talk about you," she says point-blank, sounding like a shrink.

We talk about me, while she dissects the tuna pizza with a disgusted expression. Performing a meticulous triage, she sets aside the crust (too thick), the egg (overcooked, this time), the olives (they have pits), and a few mushrooms she had not anticipated.

"I don't understand," she apologizes. "Usually their pizzas are quite good."

I agree, hoping she will move on. But although hope springs eternal, it often does so in vain.

"I don't believe this, the guy must be on vacation."

Intrigued, I keep an eye on her plate as she rather distractedly tends three little piles of food with her fork: one pile of rejects, one pile to pick from occasionally, and the pile she is sorting, supplying the first two. Sometimes she breaks eye contact with me to manage her dissection, because each ingredient must be assigned to its proper place. An olive? Garbage. A long strand of mozzarella? The edible pile. It is unbelievable what free people can do with a simple pizza.

I have hardly touched mine. I don't feel well, squeezed in elbow-to-elbow with other patrons who laugh and talk loudly, drinking and smoking. It's getting stuffy in here, and I can't help thinking about all this waste, all this food that will wind up in huge trash bags, all these plates picked over by people who like this but don't like that, aren't hungry anymore, find the eggs badly cooked.

Abandoning to the waitress a plate filled with the debris of the open-pizza operation, the journalist announces that she still has room "for a teensy dessert."

"How was it?" asks the waitress.

"Very good," says the woman, who in the last half hour has talked more about her pizza than I have about my prison.

"Their crème brûlée is super," she tells me.

I will be skipping dessert. I wasn't even hungry in the first place, and I am not one of those people who can eat without an appetite. I have to have stomach cramps and a slightly dizzy feeling of emptiness before I can eat anything. Basically, I have to be in food withdrawal, like a drug addict. In this world of freedom where I now live, the only thing lacking is a lack of anything. But then I remember that in this world, people will never have enough time, not even the time to know there's anything missing.

I realize for the first time that the virulence of my judgments has diminished. Perhaps I'm finally on the right track . . . One day I'll be able to understand these people, even to defend their ways. Who knows? Maybe one day someone will look at me the same way I look at them now. It's just a matter of time. Funny how it all comes back to the idea of time . . .

So I take my time in the pizzeria. I would like to take the food I have not eaten home with me, along with everything the other patrons will not be eating. Stockpiling is second nature to me: I am like a squirrel, daily packing away stores for leaner times—which never arrive, at least not in the privileged milieu in which I now live, so the stashes I have hidden in the back of the fridge or the cupboard always end up in the garbage. Out they go, the half-slice of quiche, the tag end of a sandwich, the half-eaten raisin muffin, the leftover pasta, everything I had carefully put away, and which no one is allowed to touch. Those provisions are mine: no one else may either finish them or throw them out. They are my hoard, my cheeks stuffed full of nuts for the winter.

"Throw out those leftover French fries," begs Eric. "They are disgusting when they're reheated."

I absolutely refuse, although I know their fate is sealed. Hoarding is stronger than I am. In a few years, I will discover the United States, that paradise for squirrels, where everyone goes home with a doggy bag, which in spite of its name almost never goes to the dogs.

When I eat at home, I'm similarly compelled to leave a little something on my plate, so that it can be added to my hoard. I don't throw it away—that would be too painful.

Every day I see swarms of boisterous kids coming out of fast-food places, their arms loaded with paper bags bursting with leftovers. McThis, McThat—people order more than they need, adding a few francs to have the "maxi" menus, the biggest Cokes, the largest fries, the extra cheeseburger. It doesn't matter whether you finish it all or not, because the difference in price is so small that you might as well jumbo-size everything and discard what is left. And if you can get a free sandwich . . . In the world of freedom, the motto is, "If it's free, take it." You can always toss it. Or just nibble on it. People are so pleased to be given something without having to reach for their wallets that there is no way on earth they will refuse an offer. And yet it's easy to do, and I have said it myself: "No, thanks, I'm not hungry enough for the extra cheeseburger." The looks I get! As though I were from Mars.

"Take it anyway, it comes with the order."

I see hamburgers, hardly touched, left in the trash baskets across the street from the fast-food outlets, along with sandwiches that someone tasted with a single bite and then abandoned. Curiously, even the homeless don't touch them. It puzzles me that hungry people would refuse to eat a leftover hamburger, as if it carried every virus in the world. There was a time when that same sandwich, with or without a bite missing, would have been the feast of a lifetime for me. We definitely live in the kingdom of waste, where even the paupers are picky about their food. True, the homeless do drink more than they eat—to numb themselves, warm up, sneak through that little door for some pleasure.

Besides, I soon realize that the homeless are not the only ones who drink: when every table is a theatrical stage, alcohol always plays the leading role. Wherever you are, from the neighborhood pancake house to Le Grand Véfour, eating means drinking. What with the apéritif, the wine, the beer, the after-dinner digestive liqueur, whatever you eat is drenched in alcohol. Any meal without it is supposed to be dreary, although I have not yet grasped what makes a meal laced with alcohol so much more fun. If I had understood that, however, then I would no longer be a prisoner liberated into a world where I cannot find any footing.

Oenologist. I hear the word bandied about.

"It's like being a sommelier," people say, "but different." More than a skill, it's a calling in its own right, and not everyone is called.

"I see," I say, but I don't. Wine leaves me particularly perplexed. People study it, sniff it, check its clarity, detect a hint of this flavor, a suggestion of that bouquet, find it perfect for the fish, or absurd for the dessert. It would take a whole dictionary to decode its jargon, plus a university degree to master its subtleties. And since free people do not like to admit their ignorance in any domain, they all stick their noses into the glass to whip up a little critique. Men usually enjoy the honor of having a splash poured into their glasses before the wine is served, a splash they then swirl around (for a reason that escapes me), snuffle at, and swish about in their mouths to give the taste buds a good soaking, all while wearing an expression of solemn inspiration. Then comes the commentary, which the entire table awaits with bated breath. It's good. It hasn't breathed enough. There's a *soupçon* of black currant. It's corked. It's a touch warm. It's perfect. It's not as good as the last time. Men of few words simply nod in silent approbation while the waiter stands there, holding the bottle in religious meditation. As far as I can tell, this ridiculous ritual always ends the same way: the wine is poured and drunk. I can't remember ever seeing a bottle sent back, yet the ritual never changes.

After all that clowning, everyone drinks up the precious beverage without paying any attention to it: a swallow with the salad, a swig with the leg of lamb, and whenever I empty my glass, someone will refill it without asking me if I am still thirsty.

Neither hunger nor thirst is important, because every mid-day and evening, the theater of the table presents the same play, in which we perform our needlessly complicated parts. If it were up to me, we would all do simple walk-ons: eat when we are hungry, drink when we are thirsty—two things that, in their perfect simplicity, have seemed precious to me for a long time.

Like all uprooted souls, I am fascinated by other people's roots, to the point of envying some Parisians I meet, people whose greatest adventure has been to move to a different neighborhood. For them, I suppose, all these inherited ritu-als simply go without saying. Bread and wine: the body and blood of that France where I am having so much trouble feel-ing at home.

The only table where I've truly enjoyed myself since being freed (if you can call a mat lying on the ground a table) was in the desert of the Atlas region of Morocco, where the Bedouin, who are sparing of words, nourish themselves in silence on a handful of dates. To my mind, they have understood the real meaning of life. I am the daughter and granddaughter of Berbers; I feel more at ease with thrift than pointless indulgence.

I feel that I too am a nomad, like the people of the dunes. Give me a little water, a few dates, and some rice on holidays, and I will be the happiest woman in the world.

9
WRITING

S urviving. I was guilty of surviving—a strange kind of guilt. And the only thing that relieved this guilt was the prospect of bearing witness, of telling the entire world that the West, and France in particular, was mistaken: Morocco was not the democracy they thought it was. The barbarity at the heart of its monarchical facade had to be exposed. Telling my family's story, which was linked to those of other political prisoners whose fates were now slowly being revealed, might help me move forward with my life. In writing *Stolen Lives*, the success of which I could not, of course, have foreseen, I exorcised the past, at least in part, but I also took up another burden: the role of victim.

To put it optimistically, as Oprah Winfrey did in words I still cherish: "You were born to be a messenger." I spent such a long time delivering a message that my mission often kept me from moving forward. Now that I have Adam, I know that

I'm through being a victim. The past is over; the future belongs to me.

Writing. For years I wrote without writing, like a ghost, and for lack of paper I engraved each word in my mind, in anticipation of the day when, far from my prison where a sheet of paper was a treasure, I would write my words again. Finally. On real paper, with a real pen, so that I could give life at last to the books floating vaguely inside me. This long literary pregnancy established a strangely intimate relationship between books and me, as if each book had patiently ripened, for twenty years, in the mind of its creator. I have invented so many of them—stories, narratives, tales, letters, episodes from my life and the lives of others—and have grown attached to every one of them, every character, every mystery, every ending.

Naturally, among the first pleasures I permitted myself was paying a visit to the holy temple of books: the bookstore. In Paris, you're positively spoiled for choice. But in the world of freedom, it turns out that even books have changed.

When my first book was published, I remember stopping on impulse at a large bookstore on the Left Bank to look for it. What was I expecting? Perhaps the bookstore of my dreams: a lovely shop decorated in warm colors, with shelves of gleaming pale wood, and a friendly bookseller who had read every last line of each book in his store. A gentleman with graying hair who might recognize me (who knows?), and who would comment sagely, with insight, on the strengths and weaknesses of my account. I do not know if such a place ever really existed while I was off in prison, or if it was only the daydream of a prisoner longing to believe in an ideal world; that bookstore no longer exists, if it ever did.

In the bookstores that actually do exist, you must always spend time inspecting the display tables. The graying gentleman may be real, but he's drowning in new releases, works by the latest victims-for-a-day, the complainers, the self-important. Am I competing with them? Alas, yes. I don't want to sell my misfortune, but the law of the market is paramount. I have to earn my place. Books are everywhere and nowhere, supply always greatly exceeding demand.

How many of us there are, all bearing witness, testifying, telling all, opening our hearts! Too many to count. Books are like everything else, so plentiful that they overwhelm us. Everyone in politics, entertainment, and public life—they've all published memoirs revealing their thoughts, baring their souls, and sharing their family photo albums or their lists of the best French songs. I feel ashamed to have joined the crowd: my own account is now lost among the latest must-reads, the exclusives, the not-to-be-misseds.

Furious, I tell myself that *my* pain is unique. Producing a book was a symbolic childbirth. Nine months of labor, with the help of author and journalist Michèle Fitoussi, gave birth to an account of which I can't quite manage to believe that I'm the heroine. For nine long and painful months I dragged things out of myself with forceps, and stared unflinchingly at scenes I had done my best to erase from memory. Three times a week, I told Michèle about the suffering and the solace. I pushed on, hiding nothing, barely stopping to breathe. We had begun our collaboration in fear of being overheard, depositing each recorded conversation immediately and securely at the publisher's, as though it were in danger of being stolen. Were we being paranoid? Maybe, but we were convinced that our phones were bugged. We used codes: "tajine" or "recipe" meant that we would meet for work.

And while we worked, certain shameful scenes I had forgotten returned to trouble me. For the first time, I spoke of my childhood as an accomplice and servant to tyranny. Like Pandora's box, the royal palace of my dreams opened, releasing memories . . . For instance, my Koran teacher, an elderly man with a haughty air, a holy man who believed in genies and chanted suras and demanded that we kiss his hand— hadn't he been the first man to see me as a woman? How far had that gone? I'm haunted by that vague, uneasy memory of a man aroused by a girl of eight. Michèle advised me to see a sex therapist, who revealed the repressed and hidden truth to me. My fears of making love, which I associate with domination, date from that time. I remembered, of course, but I had wanted to forget.

Far from feeling relieved, as though I had unburdened myself, I realized that I'd unleashed the fear that has tormented me for twenty years, the fear of my persecutors and their reprisals. Even though I am now far from my jailers, shielded by the media, I'm afraid everything could collapse around me in an instant. What exactly am I afraid of? I don't even know myself. Certain terrors are so deeply rooted that they defy all logic. Even now, I sometimes wake up in the middle of the night, in those eerie hours when you can't quite tell whether you are awake or still dreaming, and I think I hear footsteps out in the hall . . . the apartment door opens and out of nowhere my jailers come to get me for crimes I haven't yet committed. Perhaps innocence begets its own guilt, planting suspicion both in oneself and in the eyes of others. That fear of being punished for things I haven't done, or haven't done yet, intensifies the hellish whirl-wind of doubt. Like a battered child, I throw my arms up over my face, warding off both blows and caresses, in order not to see what awaits me . . .

But deep down I know that telling my story is an essen-tial part of my rebirth. To exist once more in the eyes of oth-ers after being stripped of my selfhood, I must speak. Write. And, yes, ask shamelessly to be loved.

So I chose willingly to return to hell, taking Michèle along as I forced open the door it took me twenty years to close be-hind me. I had almost no identity of my own. When my con-fessions began, I no longer knew who I was. To whom could I say: I didn't dream about my father, but about Hassan II? I woke from such dreams feeling dirty, shameful. I couldn't share this with my family: they would not have understood. They hadn't been brought up at the palace, as I had. Sometimes I was even convinced that the King had simply been negligent, ignoring his responsibilities as my protector and adoptive father, when instead I should have hated him! Michèle, who was so different from me, knew how to put me at ease, embracing these conflicting feelings like a midwife of thoughts and words. Our meetings were a shelter from the world, a refuge where I sometimes arrived deeply discouraged. We would drink tea; her children Léa and Hugo would interrupt us merrily. In my solitude, I was surrounded by life.

Sometimes, having lost track of time and place, I would arrive late, upset because the door to her building had changed location, or a bus stop had secretly moved from one street to the next. Michèle nicknamed me "Mongolita." Once I'd gotten started, I poured everything out in a jumble, neglecting the details on which Michèle placed so much importance. "Only facts," she chided, half-smiling and half-exasperated. She knew I was a lunatic! We also laughed, sometimes to the point of tears, at what the two of us were going through to keep our sense of humor. We were writing this book together so that I would no longer be General Oufkir's daughter, the victim, the imprisoned Cosette, the princess torn from her slumber at the palace. I truly needed someone to help me, because I never would have managed alone. I had tried to write, hundreds of times, producing bits and pieces of text, but the difficulties were always too much for me.

Michèle is a woman of accomplishment, in full bloom, a committed journalist, an editor at *Elle*, the mother of Hugo and Léa. In spite of many setbacks, she has made a life for herself, a real one. Perfectly at ease with herself, her femininity, and the choices she has made, she possesses everything that I lack. I see in her what I might have been, if only I'd had the chance.

FREEDOM

After the writing came success: in France, then Europe, then America, and around the world. Whenever I went to see my Parisian publisher, I could spend a full fifteen minutes just looking at the window display: there was my book, and in the middle of the cover, that photo of the six of us, such young children, with haunted eyes. Success hasn't changed me, far from it, but it has let me emerge from anonymity. Public reaction, readings, everything came at once, a rush of reaching hands. Had it all come too late? Why hadn't some editor, politician, or seasoned feminist spoken out earlier, when we'd needed them?

When I think about my readers, I cannot really say what motivates them: compassion, a simple thirst for information, curiosity, a touch of voyeurism . . . Perhaps reading about my ordeal somehow relieves the petty frustration of their daily grind. At the book fairs, as I sat behind my little table, they came to catch a glimpse of my pain. I remember an old Moroccan man in Montpellier who even offered me a rug! Perhaps he was moved by nostalgia for the name of Oufkir . . . Elsewhere, I was interrogated as though I were Mother Teresa and knew the magic spell for escape, or held the charm against suffering. At times, victims of other, even more corrupt regimes challenged me as though we were all in a competition to see who had suffered the most.

My success is something that I experience not so much as a writer, but as a woman. No one knows better than I that my book might well have been a film, a television documentary, a magazine or newspaper article. It's my testimony that counts, and it causes a stir because it takes on a regime, a government, and above all, a king. Despite the anguish of my fear, I am thrilled to feel like a regicide, and I hope that Hassan II had time to read my words before he died. I am told that he did. And even if he did not read them, his spies certainly informed him that somewhere in the world of freedom, the woman he thought he had silenced forever was making her voice heard. Literally, as well as figuratively.

At my first public appearance, words are simply beyond me. I am petrified, a real statue of salt, but at the same time I am captivated by the magic of speaking out and being heard.

I wring my hands convulsively, and my stomach is in knots. Emerging from the microphones, my voice sounds bizarre to me, metallic, not to mention childish, tremulous and shy. But the magic works anyway. The audience listens in the deepest silence, with such attention that I can almost feel it in the air. They listen. See me. Respect me. And I am reborn. I exist. Yet I am the same woman who has been flagrantly ignored for months, to the point that simply having coffee at a sidewalk table becomes a torment. With each word, I feel life surging through me. How astonishing it is, this sensation of coming back to life, of uttering one's first cry at the age of forty-four, and above all, of being excited at the idea of beginning all over again! For I am not merely going on, I am beginning again.

I am so grateful to those many readers, all those souls unknown to me, who gave me the chance to tell my story. Even today, especially in Morocco, I run across people who smile at me, approach, and say quite simply: Thank you. I don't know what to reply, but I'm always deeply moved, as though each time were a unique experience. And, of course, it is.

Then come the radio and television interviews, which are all different, even though what I say is always essentially the same. I talk for two hours during one long discussion, relating once more how I have come to be there, answering rapid-fire questions before a studio audience as quiet as if they were attending a play. Although not as impressive as press conferences (those long sessions where you are speaking solo, surrounded by a reverent silence), the discussions paralyze me with the possibility that my interlocutors might turn aggressive. What would happen if one of them began to denounce me, to roundly defend the cause of my tormentors, or even to accuse me of lying? I would fall apart, I just know it. Luckily, to this day no one has succeeded in shaking my fragile self-confidence.

The first minutes of such events are always terrible, with my insides cramping from stage fright. The other participants sit down and relax, glancing at me as if they already know what they are going to ask me. To them, this is a game, while for me it is a public disrobing, a kind of shock-psychoanalysis, broadcast live. Each time I must resist the impulse to run away from the microphone, the debate, the audience, and, most of all, their eyes. As my words pour forth, almost out of control, I no longer see individual faces beyond the stage or fear the hostility of the other participants; my breathing becomes regular, and my heart stops trying to burst out of my chest. In short, I tame my anxiety, I control my fear. I get through the interview.

"Next week, you'll be doing a book signing," the editor tells me. "It's not very exciting, but everybody has to do it."

A book signing. Nothing to worry about (I tell myself) for someone who has just been baptized by the fire of nonstop interviews and talk shows, which are the nightmare of every self-respecting introvert.

And off I go to the book signing like a French soldier heading to the front in 1914, jaunty and unsuspecting. Because the book signing venue is an arena where authors—depending on their predisposition—play the role of a bull, or a rather ill-equipped gladiator, or even, if they are truly unlucky, the martyr thrown to the lions to amuse the populace.

"You see, all these people are here for you!" the editor exclaims with enthusiasm, no doubt thinking to reassure me.

"Really?"

"Unless they think you're the cashier, I do believe they are waiting on line for you to write a dedication in their books."

"All of them?"

"All of them."

We haven't even stepped through the doors of this imposing bookstore and I'm ready to bolt. All those people in

116

there have come to see me? That is anything but good news, because they are of all ages and sizes, from the impeccably dressed lady with a choice apartment in a posh neighborhood to the flat-broke young student in threadbare jeans. Some faces are Moroccan through and through, an obvious audience for my story, but there are also some gentlemen with bristling mustaches who look almost ridiculously French, and there is a group of Americans (have they really read the French text?), plus a woman with a whole squadron of kids who must be dying of boredom here, surrounded by books without any pictures. Are they all interested in me, in what I have to say? I can't believe it. Maybe they are just hoping for some lurid revelations about the regime, spicy new details about Hassan II. Why didn't I think of that before? I have often noticed that these anonymous ants with their hyperactive lives are huge fans of "people" magazines, where they can read up on crowned heads and their doings, the fate of kings and the revels of royals, all in the privacy of public waiting rooms. This princess has been sleeping with her bodyguard; that prince was seen rolling a hashish cigarette . . . Readers learn who has been cheating on whom, who prefers Ibiza to Saint-Tropez, who is homosexual—royalty is so tantalizing that the most innocent sunbathing shot can become the scoop of the year. And at the moment, that is what I am afraid people are expecting from me—a (slightly unusual) exposé of the secret life of the seraglio: "From the Inner Circle of the King of Morocco"; "The Unknown Hassan II"; "A Princess No Longer." I do know things, naturally. I have bared my soul and told my life story, but if they want anything more, if they are only interested in palace gossip, they will be disappointed in my book. I have never attacked my country. Morocco has remained for me a magic land, from which I draw my strength. I have accounts to settle only with its King.

"Please sit down," murmurs the torturer in charge of this execution. "Would you like a glass of water?"

I turn toward this unknown person in surprise. Is he the owner of the bookstore? I do not know, my heart is beating too fast. I do not want to sit down or have a glass of water. If I had wanted to drink some water, I would have done so at home, in private, without all these prying eyes watching my every move. My fear of other people surges back, the prisoner shoves the author aside, but with a mighty effort, I do not dash off to grab the nearest taxi.

The towering stacks of books on the table are a laughable defense against my demons. Slowly, carefully, I slide to one side of my chair, so that one of the towers is between me and the waiting people, but nothing can completely hide me from their eyes, and I don't dare lift up my own because the line is so long. I look down, seeing only the jostling bodies, the hands reaching out to me.

I have barely sat down when a nasal voice says, "To Christelle and Dadou!"

"What?"

Standing there is a young woman of about twenty, clutching a copy of my book to her breast as if someone wanted to snatch it away.

"The dedication: To Christelle and Dadou."

Christelle and Dadou will park my book on their book-shelves, proud of these few hastily scribbled words: "Best wishes, M.O." Best wishes, as the formula goes, as if we were old friends. Best wishes . . . It is the disembodied friendship of the great media game. A few words scrawled on an almost blank page, just below the "real" dedication, and *voilà*: I am now their old friend.

"You look like you're in pretty good shape," one man re-marks; he seems surprised, perhaps even a little disappointed.

I almost feel I should apologize for not being the concentration-camp wraith he had expected to see. And I begin looking up into those eyes looking down at me, eyes opened wide as if to capture my attention. Some people are there to show me their support; others wish to satisfy a sometimes un-healthy curiosity. I am grateful to the first, and even to those others, for through them I exist: sometimes for real, sometimes for show, by turns encountered in the flesh or merely imagined, but always alive, and that alone justifies everything.

Eventually I get used to book signings, just as I did with mi-crophones. Sometimes ghosts appear to darken my mood, lin-gering for a few hours, even a day or two. These malevolent shadows deny my experience, rage about lies or exaggera-tions, reject the slightest accusations against the King as the worst kind of calumny. Beware of criticizing idols.

They are always Moroccans who have left their country behind deliberately and now, far from Casablanca, feel compelled to defend it with shrill patriotism. In France and elsewhere, these fighters for justice spew a revisionist line that freezes my blood: my father becomes a torturer, while his executioners are nowhere to be seen, and I am a propaganda tool in the pay of this or that cabal. There are only a handful of these specters among all my readers, but they are the ones who leave the deepest mark on me, for their convictions are like red-hot burns in my flesh. Nothing is worse than such denial, the shrug of a man who knows nothing, thinks he knows the truth, and seeks to sweep away twenty years of suffering as though they had never existed.

The book fair in Geneva is not much different from the one in Paris; I have the familiar feeling of being crushed beneath tons of books, of drowning in an ocean of humanity so dense that faces are only a blur. Where are my friends, my editor, my publicist? Where is Eric? Somewhere in the crowd. Close by, perhaps, but I would never see them anyway.

Each big publishing house strives to have the most eye-catching publicity, with huge posters and banners. One company sets up a vast dome, while another has a dazzling light-show, because the idea is to be seen from afar, to attract sales. From the table where I have been seated to sign a pile of my books, I can even make out a sort of revolving minaret somewhere in the middle of the crowd.

Tossed ashore by the sea of gawkers, a couple stops to study me as though I were an animal in a cage. It would hardly surprise me if they tossed me some peanuts. Without concealing their curiosity, the couple tries to read the title of my book—which isn't hard, since there are twenty of them on the table.

"Who's this?" the woman asks.

"You know, that female bandit," the man replies, lowering his voice, but if you want to be heard at this book fair, you are going to have to shout, period.

"Who did you say?"

"The Indian woman . . . No, you remember, we saw her on TV . . ."

Watching them cling to one another and sneak looks at me, a little embarrassed but unable to resist their curiosity, I wonder which of us is really in the cage. Finally the man gives me a smile that is more like a grimace, and drags his wife off by the arm.

"Come on, I see Sullitzer, over there."

I can still hear their voices for a moment: "What Indian woman? I don't remember!"

"Yes you do—the poor woman who got herself raped . . . in India . . ."

"Oh, right! Well, my goodness, how thin she is . . ."

The Indian woman in question was on the front pages of newspapers at about the same time as I was; they devoted a segment to her on the day when I was invited to be interviewed on the nightly news. Raped, scorned, that young woman retreated to a mountain village where she took over a gang and launched a veritable guerrilla war against the establishment. A female Robin Hood, she was fighting—as I recall—for the cause of women, for her own honor, and perhaps for some less noble reasons as well. Side by side in the same news program, she and I have now gaily become indistinguishable from each other, because in the free world, the victims of suffering are interchangeable.

10
HOMELAND

"Morocco: Kingdom of a Thousand Flavors." For a few days now, this slogan has been cruising around on the side of every bus in Paris, emblazoned across a background of minarets, sand dunes, white-washed houses, and streets blazing with colors. The first time I saw the posters, I stood transfixed, watching the Medina drive away on the rear end of a bus. Memories that I thought had gone numb returned violently to life, like a bout of nausea; memories that are now stirred up at every street corner, when I notice my country sailing down the Boulevard Saint Germain. Ten times a day, I see the same slogan over different images: camels in the sunset, a souk, a palm grove. And the eternal couscous steaming on its copper table, a mouth-watering image for drivers caught up in traffic.

Since I arrived in France, I've been constantly urged to trumpet my hatred of Morocco, the country that killed my father, shattered my family, and stole my youth. In the world of freedom, life is like the evening movie on TV: there are the good guys and the bad guys, and the latter are usually punished at the end, except perhaps when they are kings of Morocco. And just as in the movies, my liberation should have a happy ending, one unsullied by the slightest shadow of nostalgia.

"What a terrible country," exclaims a friend of a friend, shaking his head solemnly.

What country is he talking about? Mine, undoubtedly, and in accents of horror, intending to please me. What does he know about Morocco, about my experience, about the light and shadow of the kingdom of a thousand flavors?

Both my father, Mohammed Oufkir, and my mother, Fatima Chenna, are descended from the Berbers of the high Atlas Mountains in Morocco. Their families were always ready with food and shelter for the hungry and the needy, who are many in this rugged, barren region. I had been raised as a princess, but I came from the people. At the market I was often told I bargained like a Berber.

I rediscovered my inner peace and my love of Morocco in the desert. I have roamed far and wide through the desert, often with my dear friend Sabah. I'm especially fond of Tafilalet, the birthplace of my paternal ancestors. This is where I came from; I can feel it. Amid the ocher dunes, the immensities of golden brown sand, the palm groves where the blue men dwell, the rule of silence is absolute. I know my roots are here. I feel profoundly Moroccan. I'm not at home at the Hotel Mamounia in Marrakesh: luxury hotels mean nothing to me. After all, I'm no longer a princess.

Nightfall finds me at Jemaa el-Fna, literally the "meeting place of the dead," the esplanade where the heads and bodies of executed prisoners were displayed in the days of the sultans. I sit on a simple wooden bench, one of a few arranged around a cheerful cook who grills skewers of chicken and prepares meat and vegetable tajines. At last, a simple cuisine. The people of Marrakesh cluster around us, and I give the delicious food out to whoever wants some, a homeless woman bent with age, a famished little girl with big eyes. Amused, I watch snake charmers bewitch the tourists. Often someone recognizes me, and a fortuneteller approaches to tell me my future. It's hardly a risky proposition!

The posters of a thousand flavors stick up above the Parisian gridlock, stretching as far as the eye can see. Drivers twist around in their seats, frantically changing the radio station, impatiently picking their noses in an effort to keep busy. One year ago, I was where they are, at the wheel of a big 4 × 4, but in the streets of Casablanca. Closing my eyes, as if lulled by the concert of car horns, I can almost believe I am back there. I can see myself, a nervous wreck, in a Moroccan-style traffic jam: noisier, more colorful, and probably more polluted than this one, because the heat and the sun increase the toxicity of the diesel exhaust. Six round trips every day, perhaps more, between a film studio and some offices, because my first job after prison was to be an all-purpose employee for an advertising agency. Very glamorous on paper, my duties meant spending most of my time in that constant traffic jam to satisfy the whims of a capricious producer. But now I have a position, a salary, a skill I picked up on the job, and even though I still can't forget that I am not yet permitted to fly off to France, where the man of my life is waiting for me, my job does bring me a precious semblance of identity.

All around me, the anthill of Casablanca is living it up in an explosion of color and light. The crowds stream along the main thoroughfares against a background of radio and television noise, shouts and laughter, a medley of sounds pouring from every window, every balcony, every shop open to the street. The whole world seems to be enjoying itself while I wait anxiously, cloistered in my 4 × 4 like a recluse. Far from finding the peace of God, however, I squirm in my seat with growing impatience, and ever-increasing hunger.

There are moments when the eyes and the stomach are as one, and so, in the midst of that tumult, the only thing I notice is the little wheelbarrow of a peddler hawking semolina pancakes about a hundred meters away. If I weren't trapped in this damned car, I would rush over for an orgy of those delicious Moroccan snacks, whose aroma seems to reach me in spite of the distance, my closed windows, and the air conditioning. As if to taunt me, two youths buy some pancakes so piping hot that they're hard to handle. I feel a little faint, while my stomach reminds me, with a series of gurgles, that an honest working woman must not forget to eat.

The light turns green, we move forward only a few meters, and there is a sudden knock on my window. I jump, more from surprise than fear, because fear has limits in Morocco, limits that I will not find later in Europe.

It is the two young men who just bought the semolina pancakes: they have crossed the street, and standing amid the sea of cars, they signal me to roll down my window.

"Here, madame," says one of them, handing me a pancake wrapped in newspaper.

Mesmerized, I take hold of the current object of all my longings.

"If we'd started eating without giving you any, we'd have felt terrible," the other youth explains to me with a smile.

Horns blare. I barely have time to stammer my brief thanks before they are off, going on their way as if nothing had happened.

That is what Morocco is, even more than it is the jails of my youth. It is two strangers who notice the hungry desperation of an anonymous driver craving a semolina pancake. It is an instant of fulfillment, the giddy feeling of not being alone in the world. Perhaps there are other lands where a simple look can say everything, and where someone cannot bear to taste his lunch without first satisfying the hunger of an unknown woman. Until I have seen those lands with my own eyes, I will love Morocco—I from whom it stole twenty years—and defend it against those who condemn it. My country is not its King.

My country is not that repressive machine manipulated like a weapon by a crowned head. My country is these people who hold out their hands to you without expecting anything in return, people so plain and true that not even the aroma of the best pancakes in the world can make them pompous and arrogant.

The shortest route to take for a visit with my family in Rabat, a few hours' drive to the northeast of Casablanca, begins by cutting through the ramparts that surround the royal palace in the center of the city. Two roads completely traverse the compound that is sacred to all Moroccans, a house that once was mine. But just the idea of driving through there upsets my stomach, and the panicky return of my worst terrors has always forced me to make long detours instead. Until the day when, impelled by an urgency that will brook no delays, I find myself once again facing the citadel of fear, determined to pass through it.

Unlike the murderer who supposedly returns to the scene of his crime, the prisoner is rarely inclined to stroll beneath the windows of his torturer. Especially when the walls are laden with memories, when they have absorbed both laughter and tears. My childhood has remained captive inside that majestic enclosure, where it stopped dead, like a broken watch.

At the foot of the ramparts, my car itself seems to hang

back, and despite my timid taps on the accelerator, it advances only slowly into the palace grounds. At the entrance, a policeman in full uniform waves me along imperiously.

"Drive on!"

I'm trying! He has no idea how hard I'm trying . . . A sign reminds me that one may not exceed twenty-five miles per hour, which seems supersonic to me, because I hardly dare touch the accelerator at all. Someone might see me, someone might hear me! Pedestrians stride past me with ease, while the cars behind me flash their lights furiously (because it is not always considered good form to beep your horn in the Ogre's house). I am dizzy, having hot flashes, feeling nauseated—just like a pregnant woman. Perhaps a window is opening somewhere, revealing a familiar face, a clear and piercing eye that would recognize me immediately, behind the tinted windows of my 4×4.

Memories are swirling all around me, sometimes joyous and sweet, sometimes bitter: the walls are coming alive, telling my story, and I, huddled in my car, watch each minute crawl by like an eternity.

A driver right on my rear bumper finally sticks his head out his open sun roof: "You sleeping here tonight or what?"

I slept here for a long time. Which is precisely why I am having so much trouble moving forward today. A few hundred meters ahead of me, a new liberation awaits: the second gate, the one through which I will leave the palace behind forever. As I draw level with the sentry box, my car slows down even more, which must truly amaze the miserable souls behind me. When the policeman on duty glances at me, I freeze almost solid, so nervous that I actually confuse my hands with my feet and stall out badly. The policeman comes over while I am frantically turning the key in the ignition like someone in a bad thriller.

"Is there a problem?"

"I stalled," I reply, hoping my sunglasses will conceal my embarrassment and my identity.

The guy walks completely around my car, while my heartbeat goes wild. Why am I so upset by this policeman, when his fellow officers have been nothing but polite to me since I was set free? I don't know. I want to get out of here. Crossing the palace grounds has destroyed my ability to think logically, and if I let my anguish gain the upper hand, I will start believing that I will never get out of here.

The policeman comes up to me confidently.

"That's the problem with Toyotas. My brother-in-law had the same trouble."

"Oh, really," I comment, in the voice of a woman about to be executed at the side of the road with a bullet through her head.

"Give it a bit of gas, like this," he says, pretending to pump the accelerator with his open hand. "It'll start right up."

The engine turns over, catches. I am breathing hard.

"You see," observes the policeman triumphantly. "Toyotas—I've got 'em down."

Seeing me tremble at every street corner, you might think that my country is a barbarous kingdom ruled by the law of the jungle. But that simply isn't so, and I almost feel angry at myself over this visceral, paralyzing fear. I know that the regime has taken advantage of Islamist attacks to impose a reform of the *Mudawana,* the ancestral family code that for centuries kept chipping away at the rights of women. Even the Leftists had always refused to annul those outdated laws, since men of all political persuasions no doubt agree on this essential point: the domination of their female companions. The government has needed all its powers of persuasion (and God knows it has plenty) to grant rights at long last to Moroccan women, under the pretext of combating religious extremism. I now put my hope in the reformist policies of our present king, Mohammed VI, even if political freedoms still have a long way to go here.

"You don't find it too difficult to be a woman in an Islamist country?" a journalist asked me when I first arrived in Paris.

"Morocco is not an Islamist country."

"Well, Muslim, then."

"It isn't Muslim, either."

Morocco is a land of Muslim traditions, most of whose citizens practice a tolerant form of Islam. From certain perspectives, my country is one of the most enlightened nations in the Arab world; in other respects, it is the equal of the worst dictatorships in the Third World. As time goes by, we will sort through the thousand flavors of Morocco, keeping only the best ones. Perhaps we would no longer have a thousand, but even a hundred would more than suffice to make my homeland a paradise—unless the bearded men get their hands on it and cover it with a black veil.

11
FUNDAMENTALISM

During my twenty-year absence, religion has set itself up handsomely. In Morocco and elsewhere, I feel its heavy presence, one tainted at times with a brutality that recalls the crusades, the pogroms, and the stake. As the free world loses its bearings, religion makes its insidious sales pitch, offering an all-expenses-paid stay in paradise (another realm of a thousand flavors) in exchange for unswerving loyalty and services. I cannot understand how the most antiquated fundamentalism came back into fashion in the space of one generation, like the bell-bottoms of the seventies. Faucets giving way to electric eyes and plastic replacing cash—I can handle that. But when people resurrect bloodthirsty and ignorant ghosts from their dusty coffins, that bewilders me. What happened to make the world once again follow the blind?

At first I thought that resurgent fundamentalism was confined to portraits of the Ayatollah hanging in the poor neighborhoods of the East, but I was wrong. Veils are flourishing on the Champs Elysées, and little boys, third-generation immigrants, are reproaching their sisters for walking around bare-headed. How long before we see girls stoned for wearing skirts?

The Paris Book Fair is in full swing, and among the people waiting impatiently to have their books signed I notice a woman with a solemn expression. With time, I have learned to recognize at a glance those who will silently hold out their books, those who will say a few words to me, and those who, embarked on a sacred mission, will launch into long monologues that I often find difficult to cut off. And this woman belongs to that last category, I would bet on it. She leans her whole upper body across the table that separates us, looks carefully to the right and left, and with the utmost caution, whispers, "How come the King agreed to adopt you even though you're Jewish?"

So I lean closer, as if to help protect our shared secret, and whisper back, "I'm not Jewish, I'm a Muslim."

Silence. She is pop-eyed with surprise.

"You're not Jewish?"

It is not really a question, more like a statement of dismay.

"No."

She nods, and her stunned expression says it all.

"Ah. Well. But I was sure that . . ."

"You were wrong."

She hesitates, then hands me her book, almost distaste-
fully. I sign it. She retrieves it, still with the same reluctance,
and something tells me that she will throw into the nearest
trash can this story by a woman she took for a coreligionist,
who is in fact nothing but a Muslim. Perhaps someday soon
books will be stamped: "Written by a Jewish woman; you may
proceed." Or: "100% Hallal; read without fear." Kosher music,
movies blessed by the Vatican—everyone's entertainment will
be personally approved by his or her god.

The danger is not a new one, and although I would not claim
to have foretold the future, I did catch a glimpse of it in Morocco in 1991, right after I was released from prison. As if to
leave behind the scenes of my childhood (and more practi-
cally, because money does not grow on trees), I moved to a
neighborhood being "gentrified," a working-class district in
Casablanca where I enjoyed rediscovering the Moroccan people. That is where I began patronizing a little video club a few
minutes' walk from my apartment in the hope of catching up
on many things I had missed, because films had not waited
around for me either, and even literary fiction had passed me
by a long time ago. This video club, modestly called Hollywood Star, was a tiny shop with a rickety sign above its premises. A chaotic jumble of cassettes, it was run by four young
brothers who lavished me with all the advice I needed, and

spared me *The Return of the Living Dead*, etc., to send me home instead with things like *Rain Man*. We became friends; they delivered cassettes to my place, and I taped films from my television set for them to add to their stock. I may even have rented some of those very films back from them, the shop was run so haphazardly.

One day, we decide that they need to implement a new classification system and buy shelves more suited to their business. Discovering my entrepreneurial side, I plan the shop's future as if I were playing Monopoly. What better distraction from my own problems than plunging excitedly into the financial strategies of the soon-to-be multinational Hollywood Star?

After a few weeks, however, managerial standards at the store have slipped again. More than once, I arrive to find the iron gate lowered, or to discover that a stack of films has disappeared into thin air.

"What's going on? Everything's a mess," I protest to the two brothers who welcome me.

"What do you expect?" says one of them. "There are only two of us now, and it's so much work."

"But where did the other two guys go?"

In reply, one of the remaining brothers simply shrugs his shoulders.

The other two are at the main mosque. Like many other young men in this neighborhood where people often go hungry, they have fallen into the clutches of fundamentalism, traded their jeans for djellabas, cut off their brown curls, and stopped shaving. The bearded men have roped them in by touting the benefits of prayer, a method as good as any other to earn money and achieve success. Serving religiously in this world to receive a hundred virgins in the next, quite a bargain . . .

The last two defenders of the Hollywood Star beg me to talk some sense into their brothers, and to return them to the bosom of international capitalism. Without their help, the shop—which was not exactly thriving even with its full complement of employees—might have to close soon. Farewell, meager earnings that support an entire family: an invalid father, a mother burdened with children of all ages, and four grandparents still on this earth, thanks be to God, as the saying goes.

"They'll listen to you. Tell them we need them here!"

I promise that I will try, even though I won't pull much weight against the fundamentalist god, or against God Himself, for that matter.

A few days later, the two bearded disciples are walking smugly down the street past the video club, cultivating an aura of wisdom that seems rather silly, since they are only about twenty-five. Our discussion does not get far, even though the recruiters at the mosque have not yet completely brainwashed them. The brothers are still speaking coherently, lapsing only occasionally into jargon. Their motivation? Commerce just isn't viable anymore . . . At the mosque, one can still find hope, in praying to God. The best is yet to come, in the next world, of course, where the martyrs are already living it up, although it is hard to lounge around wearing those awkward belts of dynamite.

"Think it over . . ."

"We have."

"Think some more!"

What else can I say? I feel the battle is lost, and we separate as good friends, but with the feeling that we will not be meeting again. With a slight pang, I remember their wild laughter in the little shop the day I asked them, in wide-eyed innocence, who "Mad Max" could possibly be. And now, even they will soon have forgotten him.

But I have gone into mourning for Moroccan youth just a little too soon. A few months later, I run into the two lost brothers again. This time they are clean-shaven, wearing jeans and T-shirts, with Walkmans clamped to their ears. When they see me coming, they break into wide smiles.

"Yeah, yeah, don't say it, we know."

After holding their interest for a while, Utopia has finally revealed its limitations, in spite of the brothers' longing for hope. Unwilling to bury their identities under an avalanche of dogma, fearing to lose touch with who they are, they have come home. End of story.

The young people of Morocco are not really searching for their identities, which may explain why fundamentalism finds less fertile ground there. Proud of their roots, young Moroccans flirt with extremes only as a sign of revolt against a cannibal system. They need only one thing: freedom. Freedom and work. And no one understands that better than I.

Hollywood Star has disappeared, God rest its soul, but under the nose of fundamentalism (and tweaking its beard), it has changed into a small supermarket, a pleasant little store, nicely arranged, and serving a healthy neighborhood clientele. I worked hard alongside the four brothers to make their shop into a viable business, and to turn their entrepreneurial spirit to good use. The accounts are looking up, the prospects excellent, and at a rough estimate, they should be turning a profit well before the end of the world—so that they can get their hands on some earthly dividends, rather than heavenly virgins. It is a short-term calculation, the wisdom of which we probably will not learn until the day of our deaths.

12
THE DESERT

Work is an inescapable fate for some, but a pleasure, a drug, a relief for others. As for me, I rediscovered work after twenty years in prison, and I think that for me it was simply a way of slipping back into a world that was no longer my own. During the years that I spent in Morocco after leaving prison and before going to Paris, my family and I were followed and watched every minute of the day, and I was the only one of us to be given back this most basic of rights: to earn a living. I plunged into the world of work with delight, putting almost everything else from my mind so I could devote myself to commercial shoots that began to resemble affairs of state. The money meant little, but I carried out every mission given to me, no matter how trivial, as though I'd been sent after the Holy Grail.

To be a professional is to *be* someone, period. I think that is what interests people most of all, and my goal is precisely to interest people, to prove to them that I belong in their world. And to do that, I spare myself no pain, no anguish, because deep down the only thing I really want is to bury myself in a hole and breathe through a straw so short no one will notice it. But of course I cannot shut myself away like that, for I have left prison behind and must never allow myself to go back.

Thanks to the intervention of some influential people in Parisian media circles, the Moroccan professional world opens its doors to me well before the country itself will let me go live my life abroad. But the Ogre's police are on the prowl, as I am still under constant surveillance, and when I start work on my first shoot, Home Security just happens to come rooting around in the personnel files. They are wary of everything and everyone: after all, it is a Franco-Italian co-production, and who knows, it could be a nest of spies, a threat to the regime, the country, the King.

An official who hides his eyes behind dark glasses tells our producer curtly that it's "a question of national security."

Everyone knows that it isn't really the Italian technicians or the French editor who are worrying the authorities, but my accursed last name. Oufkir, a synonym for silence and oblivion. Even today, that name cracks like a gunshot—and gunfire attracts the police, whose sole desire, as everyone knows, is to restore order. An Oufkir has no business working—

freely—on a commercial shoot, still less coming into contact with foreigners. Silence is the weapon of dictators.

By hanging around the set more tenaciously than a clutch of groupies, the Home Security thugs have inspired an atmosphere of tension hardly conducive to work. Fear, albeit a picturesque feature of Morocco, does not much motivate the crew's foreign contingent, who feel oppressed by the mood of vague, inarticulate menace. As for the Moroccan producer, he is in a paroxysm of hysteria, and despite his initial warm welcome to me, he finally fires me with a slew of lame excuses.

"You're too inexperienced," he says, closing the file on me without daring to look me in the face. "And besides, our budget has been cut."

I am so angry I'm almost choking. After stealing twenty years of my life, they are stealing my right to work (I don't dare say my "reintegration into society," which would make it sound as though I had committed a crime). All sorts of outside pressure will have to be brought to bear once more to get me back my job.

"It's so nice to have you with us again," the producer lies, forcing himself to smile.

I know for a fact that he was obliged to take me on again, and that threats of financial reprisals have won out over threats of ordinary reprisals. I am working, true, but only because someone has been compelled to employ me. In those conditions it is difficult to blend seamlessly into the group and imitate my colleagues' devotion to their work. It is also difficult, once I get over the humiliation of being fired and then rehired as a result of conflicting pressures, not to have sympathy for those who are oppressed by the system. Everywhere we shoot, every time we change locations, the crew finds itself cluttered with policemen, Home Security agents, and political police. As production supervisor, I must obtain any required authorizations from the governor, the state police, or the *caïd* (a title which, despite its connotation of oriental intrigue in the West, is the Moroccan equivalent of "mayor"), and these requests, signed "Oufkir," give more than one poor fellow quite a start.

Night falls quickly in Casablanca, and after a long day of work, all I want is to go home. A few streets away from my place, however, a large black BMW is parked right in the middle of the street. I honk once, without success. I honk again, and then again, trying to remind the driver that he is blocking the way. Suddenly, the car door opens and a man gets out in a menacing manner. From his macho mustache, that inimitable set of his shoulders, and in spite of his well-cut civilian suit, I recognize the type: a soldier, the regime's guard dog. He proves me right by hurling abuse at me, waving his military papers under my nose.

"You have no idea whom you're dealing with!"

Oh yes I do, and how. The whole paradox of Morocco is there, precisely, in that abuse of power that forms such a violent contrast with the sense of compassion and solidarity characteristic of my people. This man is a colonel, and like all officers he imagines himself invested with an almost royal power, so of course he threatens me with the worst. The worst? If only he had the slightest idea of what I have been through.

When I get home, for the first time I use whatever pull I have to make sure that the man with the BMW pays for bristling his mustache at me. I simply cannot bear the abuse of power any longer, and even if I must dabble in it myself to put a miniature torturer in his place, I will do anything to avoid having to deal with such people.

A lifetime ago, puffed up with her father's power, the seventeen-year-old daughter of a police officer had me thrown out of a movie like a tramp. I shrugged it off, because I was a different person back then, still unwilling to bring the ultimate injustice into play. At the time I was reluctant to live off my name. With a single word, the all-powerful General Oufkir could have reduced her policeman father to a dishrag, and perhaps just knowing that was enough for me. But now my father is no more, those petty bullies have poisoned every minute of my stolen youth, and no one is ever going to step on my feet again.

After three and a half years of hard work, I am beginning to think that doors are finally opening not through influence and

151

threats, but simply because people recognize my professional worth. Courageously, my new boss has not been intimidated by pressure from on high: he met with me, listened to me, and put me to the test. All he cares about is the value of my work. I am moved to tears; I have been shifted around for so long, like a bundle that is always in the way.

"I am hiring you for what you can do, and nothing else. Got that? Nothing else. Besides, if you turn out useless, I'll fire you!"

At that instant, I feel like a new woman, or is it that I have never been so much myself?

But prison still weighs on me like an invisible shadow. Despite the welcome professional pride I take in my job with the advertising agency, I remain uncomfortable around lots of people, and the atmosphere on the sets begins to exhaust me with its noise, lights, bright colors, shouting, and stress. Many times I have felt like jumping into my car and driving anywhere just to get away from it all. While it is true that solitude awakens my ghosts, it's even more true that crowds depress me.

I find my middle way by accident, during a shoot in the Atlas desert. The sun is already so strong in Rabat that we are told to expect horrendous temperatures when we reach our location. Leaving the city in my equipment-laden 4×4, I have no idea that with each kilometer, I am drawing closer to serenity. Our destination is Erfoud, a kind of Hollywood desert à la Morocco. A tourist seeking exoticism would be ecstatic: all the American superproductions requiring vast, empty spaces and any kind of desert ambience are shot there, next to spare, sun-baked villages one visits by camelback. It's *Lawrence of Arabia*, as far as the eye can see. Erfoud has become an enormous machine, an open-air studio as big as the desert, where the endless sand periodically becomes a parking lot for trucks, antennas, tents, control rooms, lights, and refrigerators. You hear a babel of languages there: Arabic and English, of course, but French and Italian as well.

"Do you mind staying with the locals?" I am asked.

"Not at all!"

I am both curious to meet these people and relieved that the tension of our journey is over. The closest village will house those of us who are not necessary to the daily shooting schedule. Since my production work is over, I can relax and enjoy these peaceful, endless vistas, where the wind is so hot I feel as if I were smoking God's own hookah. The air makes me dizzy, and I open my arms to feel the desert wind flow deliciously through my clothes.

The woman who welcomes me could have been born a thousand years ago. There is nothing of the modern world in her garments or her weather-beaten face; her eyes are pale from too much light, and her brown hands are smooth, as if polished by the sand. When she invites me into the soft twilight of her mud-brick home, I feel as if I were going backward in time. We have tea together, take our meals together, and even share the silence, sitting on rugs as the sun goes down. I show up less and less often at the "crew table," that impressive daily cold buffet of light summer meals, fresh fruits, and pastries. I feel so comfortable with my host family that I spend most of my ample free time with them, whenever I am not needed on the set.

"So you've really settled in at the Erfoud Hilton," the producer remarks with pointed irony.

We are far indeed from minibars stocked with minibottles, king-size beds that could accommodate three fatties sleeping sprawled out like starfish, and marble bathrooms provided with paper toilet-seat protectors. The desert does not bother with accessories. Even the bare essentials are missing, and strangely enough, they prove superfluous there.

"How do you manage without air conditioning?" people ask me in the pleasant coolness of the production offices.

"You have to be there to believe this, but you don't need it."

I don't need anything, actually. And certainly not my worries, which have vanished into the desert wind, apparently intending to leave me in peace during my entire stay in Erfoud.

Desert people say very little. With time, however, my hosts and I have grown to like one another very much, and we discuss our quite different views on life and the world. The woman of the house has become my friend. She has four daughters to feed, plus her husband and his mother, who was once the most beautiful woman in the village, according to her daughter-in-law. Today, the wrinkled old lady hardly budges from the coolest corner in the house, where she sorts through great bags of lentils, picking out the tiny stones.

After a while, I ask them what they think of these strangers and foreigners who regularly invade their land, using "their" desert as a theater backdrop. I feel that I know my hosts so well that I could almost answer my own questions. Strangers? They hate them, naturally. I would swear to it. I am no doubt the only exception to this severe judgment—I, who have shown myself to be so open to their culture. Give me a little time, and I would wind up the only survivor of the inevitable massacre they would unleash if the film crew happened to go too far in violating their sacred land.

But the Friend of the Bedouins is in for a shock. No, my hosts do not hate the strangers. They hate them so little that they are disappointed that they were not asked to be in our film! Because the husband and wife, four daughters, and even the grandmother have already appeared in the credits of a good twenty American movies. Need any extras? The village is always open, and its inhabitants love to bring bustle to the background of a shot. The pay is good (everything is relative), the atmosphere is pleasant, and you meet people, people who give you little things. What's wrong with that? Especially since life is not always easy in the desert, and resources are meager.

I have not yet recovered from my surprise when they bring out a bundle of trinkets, key rings, cigarette lighters, caps, T-shirts—often stamped with the logo of a "major production." My family proudly explains that they have played in this or that film, with such-and-such an actor (whose name they mangle a bit)—and there isn't even one television in the village!

So my friend the woman of the desert, who radiates frankness and authenticity, this woman whom I believed to be completely untouched by the voluntary slavery of the free world, would be the absolute envy of all the starlets who haunt casting calls seeking work as extras in a superproduction. My hosts, in all their simplicity, are old hands at Hollywood.

"That surprises you a little," my friend says with a naughty smile.

And I suddenly realize that she has understood in an instant what was going through my head. Perhaps she is used to being a picturesque puppet for every film technician passing through. How many of them, as I will, take photos of her to show their friends how much the desert people live in another world?

"You know, one of my daughters is married to an Italian," she adds, to finish me off.

I can't help smiling.

"I thank God in all my prayers, and if it is His will, the three others will also marry foreigners."

"*Inshallah*," I reply. "God willing!"

It was only then that I really began to discover these people, with their paradoxes and contradictions. They are caught between two epochs, using one to cope with the other, without losing any of their generosity or their integrity. They are straightforward, intelligent, warm-hearted, and reserved. During my stay, my private demons were never once awakened, and I was able to live in peaceful communion with the villagers. The desert is a cocoon for me, a space far from the critical eyes of my fellow men, where I can relax and breathe freely. When the crew packs up and leaves, I know that I will come back to the Atlas desert, because the world is too small for us to neglect the only places where we feel truly alive.

A few months later, I return to the Atlas with great joy, this time in the context of a humanitarian mission. Accompanying Pharmacists Without Borders, I tour the region to educate the inhabitants about the problem of trachoma, an eye disease that can lead to blindness if left untreated. After a rather tiring journey, we enjoy two weeks sleeping under the desert sky, weeks that refresh my glimpse of an ideal world both intense and tranquil, the only landscape—and one of otherworldly beauty—where I have found peace of mind.

The village where we stay is as dry, rough, and sublime as its inhabitants. When the sun is at its zenith, the contours of the buildings melt into a startling vision, as fluid as a mirage. After my twenty years in prison, the irony is delightful: I am in charge of giving civics lessons to the women and children, who are the loveliest I have ever seen. Their skin is a coppery color, and their large, light-colored eyes devour us with curiosity. When their class is over (they listen to me for an hour and a half, these people who are so sparing of words!), the one for the men begins, and I am touched by the attention they give me. They do not care who I am, or who my father was, or who my contacts are. They value the time I am devoting to them because they are the ones being helped. Did I have to bury myself in the heart of the desert to finally find respect?

The women's ample clothing protects them not from the disapproving gaze of a misogynous god, but from the ferocious desert heat. The men's headscarves snap in the wind like the billowing canvas of our tents. I feel both empty and serene: life has made me a child of the desert, something I understood after the first few kilometers of our journey into this boundless universe where the rocky landscape gorges itself on heat and silence. A wounded soul heals faster here than anywhere else, perhaps because here the senses take over from words.

Sitting in groups on the low walls, the village women seem to have felt my fascination for their world, because they greet and bless me whenever I approach them. Have they also read my soul as if it were an open book? Be that as it may, one of them rises and comes over to me, holding a little girl in her arms.

And now she holds out to me that tiny, breathtakingly beautiful creature.

"Look, she's my daughter. My eighth daughter."

"She's lovely," I say, not to flatter her, but because the child looks like an angel from heaven.

"She is one year old."

I nod.

"Take her," says the woman. "Take her with you."

Shocked, I try to explain that I cannot take her daughter away with me. But in my heart of hearts, an old wound reopens, the pang of a motherhood that I have not known.

"Take her, save her—I have nothing to keep her alive. Save this one, at least!"

I am so confused . . . I am not thinking about the fate of this girl with her almost ash-blonde hair, deeply tanned face, and huge blue eyes, but about my own abandonment, my often-absent mother, and my desire to have a child myself.

"I felt that you would take her," the woman continues. "I sensed that in you . . ."

As in a dream, I take the child in my arms, but just as I begin to consider the idea, the little girl begins shrieking in terror, writhing in my grasp and sinking her tiny nails into my wrist.

"I can't," I tell the mother, handing back the child. "She prefers your love to her comfort."

"She would get used to you!"

"No, I can't."

The child has chosen the desert, and if I could, I would

do the same. I, too, would have liked an ordinary childhood, far from the splendor of the palace and the specters of prison, a childhood spent nestling in the loving arms of a mother. Neither princess nor prisoner, just a little girl who asked only to be comforted so that her nightmares would go away.

Without a backward look, I return to my tent, leaving behind the child who, through a sudden impulse, might have become my daughter.

13

MOTHERHOOD

I will never be a mother. Infertility: the word has the terrible weight of a sentence passed on my life, a guillotine blade fallen on my dreams. Prison left me with an absolute obsession with motherhood, almost as if bearing a child were the only way for me to become a complete woman. I tried everything with Eric: from hormonal treatments, to artificial insemination and in vitro fertilization, ovulation kits and consultations with the most respected specialists, such as Dr. René Friedmann. Every Wednesday, Eric and I went to Liège so one of my sisters could make me a present of her eggs. After that experience, the mere sight of a sign saying Liège nauseated me and set me shivering. For three years, I submitted to a marathon of exhausting treatments whose psychological toll was disastrous. At certain moments after the publication of *Stolen Lives* I felt so little suited for motherhood that I wanted to put an end to my marriage. I harbored self-destructive, almost suicidal tendencies. But we held together, Eric and I. I have forgiven those who stole twenty years of my life for everything but this: prison has kept me from being a mother.

"If those people really did kill you, then they're killing you twice over," says my gynecologist, who must have skipped the classes on the proper bedside manner when he was in medical school. Then, seeing my devastated face, he adds, "But you can always adopt, you know."

I know that. One day Nawal, my niece, will also know that. I haven't told her anything yet. For the time being, I struggle alone with my feelings of guilt, even though this child taken from her mother seems happy at my side. I am not her mother, and I am not certain I can ever become her mother someday. Her real mother, my sister Myriam, who has suffered epileptic seizures ever since our prison days, has been bounced from one hospital to another, and is in such poor health at present that she can't care for her child. The father lives in Rabat but is unfortunately often absent. What was I to do when Nawal called me Mama, and Eric Papa? I had to teach her that she had two mothers and two fathers. Naturally, the feelings of guilt that overcame me were in part assuaged by the fact that the child needed a stable home. I became her guardian in France, and her parents granted me custody of this pretty, mischievous, and lively little girl with curly hair.

Will I ever manage to forget that the child sleeping with clenched fists in the bedroom at the end of the hall isn't mine? Will I, who feel so dried up inside, have enough love to give her? I have read obscure theories about the maternal instinct that say it develops gradually during a pregnancy, coming to term along with the baby after nine months. So, no pregnancy, no love, and every adopted child becomes Oliver Twist.

"Don't be silly," says my doctor with a shrug. "Those fears are all in your head. Believe me, you have no idea how many women abandon their children at birth, even though they've carried them for nine months."

I know he's right. But I still keep wondering why I don't feel this love. One thing is certain: the clock ticks relentlessly for all women, but I'm afraid that mine will never tell time correctly again.

It's raining out on the grand boulevards of Paris, and I hurry, clutching Nawal's hand. I have never liked coming home after nightfall in midwinter. The child has spent the day at her mother's, as her solemn little face shows. The faster we get home, the quicker it will all be forgotten: the miniature uprooting each time she visits, the trip that seems so long, the endless rain . . . That's when I glimpse, in the reflections of the wet shop windows, the hulking form of a man following us closely. At first I simply keep track of him out of the corner of my eye, but it soon becomes clear that he really is dogging us. When I speed up, so does he, keeping his shoulders hunched, his head down, as if filled with evil intentions. I sense his presence, coming nearer. My heart begins to pound, and I grip Nawal's hand as if he were going to grab it from me, while my other hand clutches my purse. In the window of a shoe store I can see him, closer than ever, with his big jacket and cap. He comes so close that I can smell his odor of stale cigarettes, and it chills me.

Keeping calm, I stop short, hoping to foil the enemy. But he proves more clever than I am, passing me as if nothing were wrong, going on his way, so that for a moment I wonder if my tendency to panic at everything might have misled me. Although I have mastered many of the social codes of the free world, I still often misread people's intentions, fleeing from uniforms to throw myself into the arms of the first pickpocket who comes along, if he seems even the slightest bit nice.

This time, though, my instinct is correct: the man has slowed down to let himself be passed in turn—and he jumps me. I feel a violent tug on my shoulder: he wants my purse. Paralyzed with fear, I cling to his quarry, because I have spent too much time without an identity, and that handbag contains my papers, my photos, my money, my house keys: in short, my life. And you don't grab someone's life like that, on a street corner. But the man disagrees and shakes me like a plum tree in hopes of making me let go.

"Let go of that bag, you bitch, or I'll rough up your kid," he spits out.

Sometimes just one word can change everything, turning prey into predator. My fear turns instantly into a fury so violent that I feel claws grow out of my fingers, and now I am a lioness, a she-wolf, a she-bear, the kind of beast that does not take kindly to threats to its young.

"Say that again?" I exclaim, and without giving him time to say anything I double him over with a well-placed knee, then push him into the shop window so hard his head bangs. And I am still hitting him with whatever I can think of—my hand, a foot, my purse. My hatred has made me the aggressor and him the victim, and I do not feel that I am defending Nawal anymore, or my purse, or my life; there is only this crashing wave of hate that could crush Paris in a heartbeat. Just as in those wretched action films that usually put me to sleep, all I see are lights, the glinting rain, and the huddled figure trying to protect himself from my blows. I am a wild animal, and I will stop when he is dead.

Finally the man runs off without his loot. It is only then that I discover Nawal lying on the sidewalk in tears, holding tight to my ankle. My hatred vanishes in a flash as I bend over to take her in my arms. A few words murmured into her ear begin to reassure her, slowly dissolving the horror of those last few minutes. I stroke her hair while she clings to me. Around us, at a respectable distance, the citizens of this world of freedom look at us as if we were exotic animals. They are surprised and almost disappointed in the unexpected outcome of the mugging: a free woman is supposed to be a victim, if only to allow a male onlooker to go home and tell a scary little story to his family. He will not mention that he was so frightened that he didn't lift a finger to help the lady in distress.

Strangely enough, the attack has opened my eyes in a way that no shrink has managed to do. Motherhood . . . Maybe that plunge into the depths of primal instinct allowed me to understand how truly I am the mother of the child I am raising, even though I had not realized it. Lionesses adopt abandoned cubs, too, nursing and protecting them as if they were their own. Now I know that one need not give birth to a child to love it, and that anyone who tries to tear Nawal away from me might just as well kill me where I stand. I also know that this child who will grow up in my care will be able to count on me until it is time for her to spread her own wings.

I am a mother, and I had no idea.

14

LOVE

My first man, the one who was going to make a "real" woman out of me, came into my life shortly after I was freed from prison.

At almost forty, I am a virgin.

Antonio is Italian, a blond Apollo with curly hair, a short beard, and oodles of charm. An actor. I meet him on a movie set where my sister Maria and I have been invited by one of my childhood friends, a cultural attaché to the embassy, whom I'd seen a few times since my release.

The movie is being shot on location in the desert by a Moroccan producer with an Italian crew. It takes Maria and me a few days to adjust; it's been a long time since we've seen so many people. When we arrived, we were greeted by the sight of the entire crew in swimsuits, sunning themselves by the pool. I was terrified, so dizzy I had to prop myself up against a column. In a few minutes, my clothes were soaked with sweat.

This getaway should be a paradise on earth for me, but I have the same feeling I've often had, since my liberation, of being an outsider. Especially here, with all these film people doing their film thing, in a milieu I'd once admired from up close as a teenager, when I wanted so much to fit in. I'm more self-conscious now than ever.

Not many people in the crew know who we are or where we're from, even if our aura of sadness makes more than a few of them wonder about us.

My sister Maria spots Antonio first.

"There's a really hot guy who's totally head over heels for you," she whispers to me the first day.

"What does he look like?"

"Blond, blue eyes, a beard!"

My sister's crazy. They're all blond, tanned, bearded, and beautiful. Why on earth would a "hot guy," as she puts it, be interested in me? The next time she sees him, she points him out discreetly. It's true, he's gorgeous, but all I can see is how greedily he's staring at me, paying no attention to anything else, as though, if he could, he'd swallow me whole.

A few days after our arrival, the producer throws a party with champagne to celebrate an actor's birthday. When I step inside the large dining room, it's already filled with people.

I'm afraid of the crowd, but I force myself to stay just inside the doorway, facing down my demons. There I am, fighting them, when someone takes my hand gently into his own. His hand's so warm I let it happen. Our fingers delicately intertwine, and then he squeezes, hard, as though to convey all the passion in the world.

I turn around, and I'm looking right at him.

It's the man Maria was talking about. His eyes are still riveted on me, with the same ardent gaze. I have the feeling that we were fated to meet, that he's been waiting for me. It's insane, I know, almost forty and I'm acting like a schoolgirl. But his eyes aren't lying. This man seems to be crazy about me. So there is such a thing as love at first sight.

Silently, he draws me toward him, but I pull back slightly. Sensing my confusion, he moves two chairs to a table outside the dining room.

We sit down. He continues staring fervently at me. Maria slips away. We stay there without speaking a word. I'm shaking so hard he takes the black cashmere sweater from his shoulders and places it around my own like a shawl. Then he puts his hand right on my belly, massaging it gently.

I continue shaking, hating myself for it, berating myself for behaving so idiotically. How could this be happening to me, me, the most "experienced" of all my brothers and sisters, the one who told them stories about my romantic adventures? How can I not even be in control of my own body? How can I be as terrified and timid as a little girl, panicked and ashamed, seesawing between fear and elation?

He doesn't move from my side. I can feel his warmth, his kindness. I tell myself again that I have to stop acting like such a fool. I've dreamed of this moment for so long; this was exactly how I pictured it happening. I have to live my dream.

Antonio brings me a glass of white wine. He makes an effort to speak to me in French.

"This will warm you up," he says.

The alcohol has the opposite effect, making me shake even harder. I'm not used to it. After my second glass, seeing the state I'm in, he gives me a cognac instead.

Instead of just trembling, now I feel on the verge of collapse. I feel ill. He gets up.

"I'll walk you back to your room," he says.

He helps me lie down on the bed, then sits quietly beside me. The little girl in me is more frightened than ever. I curl up.

He crouches at the foot of the bed and looks at me for a long time.

"Who are you?" he asks me. "Where are you from? I've never seen such sad eyes . . ."

I'm frozen. I sigh, hiccup, and then start sobbing. He stays by my side until dawn. I press myself against him, and all I do is weep.

Finally, in the morning, I fall asleep. When I wake up, he's gone.

Where am I from, Antonio? From a dark, frigid place, where I've finally given up hope of ever knowing love. Of course, like all the girls of my generation, I've had a few flirtations, but never anything serious. Sometimes I even thought I was in love.

I almost got engaged to a charming young man I met as

a student in Paris. We continued to write each other during my captivity in the prison in Tamattaght, when my family and I were still able to get mail, before we were buried alive. But I soon stopped writing him; despite his love letters, he understood nothing about our situation.

Men have taken me into their arms and whispered sweet nothings. I've known the languorous pleasure of a slow dance, and what it's like to kiss a boy on the lips.

Leila Chenna was a young woman of great beauty, the favorite actress of Algerian director Muhammed Lakhdar-Hamina, who won the Palme d'Or at Cannes for his 1975 film *La Chronique des Années de Braise* (*Chronicle of the Years of Fire*). She was also my cousin, and in Paris she introduced me to Alain Delon and Jacques Perrin. I'd enjoyed brief, casual flirtations with them; I was probably a little in love with them both. They respected the young lady I was, full of virtuous principles, mindful of her honor, even though what I loved more than anything else then was singing and dancing. But I wasn't yet ready to belong to anyone. All I knew for sure was that some day in the not too distant future, I was going to get married.

That was so very long ago.

In prison, I had firmly resolved, if ever freed, to throw myself at the first person who came along, in order to satisfy my desires. Reality is more complicated. Who wants to have anything to do with a frightened old virgin? I was good for nothing but scrap, before I'd even been used.

I'd had plenty of time to imagine, in all his variations, the man who would put an end to my long sexual drought. Depending on my mood, he was a Prince Charming, a living doll, a feisty tough guy, a Foreign Legionnaire, a Bengal Lancer, a Doctor Without Borders, a blue-eyed Bedouin, a White Russian, or a redskin. A mixture of James Bond, Tarzan, and Doctor Zhivago (without the mustache, because that was the mark of a jailer).

But each night, when I told my stories, in order not to disappoint my audience or myself, I insisted on true love over carnal pleasure. How many nights, alone in that dark cell, on that ratty mattress, did I dream of making love only to wake saddened and embittered in the morning? I soon learned to stop thinking about it, or at least to think about it less often, for fear of hurting myself even more deeply.

Over twenty years, I've forgotten little by little what it means to be a woman, desirable and desired. I don't know how to smile, laugh, or dance for a man who looks at me with longing in his eyes. I no longer know the arts of seduction. My body seems to have lost its primary function: I am no longer a woman, just an eating, drinking, sleeping, walking machine. A body . . . I barely think of myself as having one.

I have to relearn everything about being a woman, from the beginning. When men turn around to check me out, my cheeks flush, my hands shake, my toes go cold—a real production, the Blushing Virgin, an act so rare these days that I would probably make a fortune in a circus. I am an old virgin, a curiosity, a museum piece. My regained freedom leaves me dizzy and oddly empty. I dream of love, desire, pleasure, but I'm afraid, and ashamed of my own fear. I'm pathetic.

Newly returned to the world of the living, I don't know how to handle myself, because when I look around me only one thing jumps out at me: sex. Sex is in the sitcoms I watch during breakfast, in the ads, at the movies, on posters and billboards where half-naked women, ethereally beautiful and cruelly youthful, display themselves for all to see. There's only one thing on everyone's minds and lips. In my absence, the world has turned, leaving even the least modest among us staggered. The flower children have been shoved aside by the culture of porn, and the so-called "sexually liberated" hippies sent back to picking daisies.

I, too, am caught up in the obsession. I want sex, and I want it now! I can't take my mind off it. If I'm honest with myself, I don't want sexual pleasure: I want, desperately, to be normal. I want to hear the coarse, tender, urgent words a man hopelessly in love with me will whisper in my ear. I want to make up for lost time.

I want to be a woman, at long last. Oh, Antonio, I'm so afraid.

Over the next few days, I try to avoid him. He takes the opposite tack, seeking me out, bombarding me with flowers, courageously playing Pavarotti and singing in Italian, dragging me off on long walks into the desert at sunset. We have a dreamy dinner for two. It's a recipe for romance, but will I fall for it?

The Italian wants to win my love, whereas I want an identity. He's put together a real masterpiece of Italian flirting, a universe of sweetness that, although not disagreeable, is aimed more at a free woman than at the floundering prisoner I am. And while he is warbling *"Ti amo"* to an eighties melody, I am wondering whether I will ever succeed in opening up, in every sense of the word.

It almost happens, once. When he realizes from the reactions of my body that I'm a virgin, I start trembling so much I can't stop myself.

He sits down heavily and begins to cry.

"What in the world did they do to you?"

I have a hard time telling him my story. Instead, he winds up telling his: divorced, two kids. At liberty.

I feel remarkably clear-headed. When he caresses me, or when I touch him, I have the impression of flipping through a dictionary, learning a new language word by word. I apply myself to the task. But without any feeling.

I watch myself going through certain motions, yet I can't feel pleasure. I can see he loves me a great deal. And I, I am in love with being in love. This must be what it's like to be a woman, I tell myself, though in fact I'm still far from the truth. For that, I will have to wait until I meet Eric, the man I will marry.

The shoot wraps up, and despite our repeated failures to connect, the Italian offers, quite seriously, to sneak me onto one of the production trucks and smuggle me out of the country. When my two brothers and one of my sisters and I broke out of our prison for six days in 1987, however, I used up all my courage for any escape attempt, leaving none left for a second try, especially since I know that the crew is infested with moles from Home Security. The Morocco of Hassan II does not look kindly on the presence of foreigners on its soil, still less when they come in contact with me.

No, I will not be escaping, to Italy or anyplace else. One day I will be officially free, with a passport in my pocket, and when that day comes, I will choose my destiny.

I go home to Rabat, to the small apartment I share with my sister Maria, certain he'll forget me.

Little did I know.

One fine morning, Antonio lands at the airport. Barely past customs, he throws himself into my arms, and is surprised by my coldness. I'm nervous because I can't make a move without being watched, but he thinks I don't love him anymore, that I've found someone else. How am I to explain the relentless surveillance that is a daily part of my life or, even worse, my constant fears of prison? How am I supposed to embrace him in broad daylight when they are all around, watching me?

Over the next few days, our misunderstandings multiply. Jealous, he makes scenes. I can't bear his shouting, his agitation, his threats. I withdraw into myself, feeling as though I were again face to face with one of my torturers.

We finally calm down. Wonderful days follow. We go to the

market together, and then Antonio takes charge of the kitchen, making pasta, fish, tomatoes with basil. He seems to bring all of Naples with him into the little apartment now filled with the smell of garlic and olive oil. He's a true actor, cheery, excitable, overflowing with life. Sometimes it's all too much for me. But he loves me, and tells me so every chance he gets.

We have lunches with Maria, on our little patio in the sun. We put on music, relax, stroll in the medina, eat out at restaurants. At night, he reassures me when it doesn't work out:

"Antonio, will I ever be 'normal'?"

"Don't worry," he says, "these things don't happen overnight."

Meanwhile, the Commander of the Faithful is on our case: Big Brother is watching us. Our little Italian island, which I had thought of as our sanctuary, is soon overrun by Home Security henchmen, who knock on our door at seven o'clock one morning. There are four of them: two who say nothing but pace around the apartment inspecting whatever comes to hand, and two others who play good cop/bad cop, as in the movies.

"Do you realize that your father, if he were alive, would not tolerate that a foreigner . . ."

My father? I can barely believe that this government tool would evoke my father, murdered by thugs like him, and put big speeches in his mouth from beyond the grave. And I can feel rage coursing through me, a rage stronger than fear, rage at this sinister ventriloquist who tries to make corpses speak.

"Please wait in the bedroom," I ask the Italian, who has no idea what is going on but would much rather be someplace else.

Now the Bad Cop, who has been lounging innocently in an armchair, starts thundering insults, calling me every name in the book—slut, shameless bitch, the disgrace of Islam—while the two mutes make themselves useful by running a tape recorder.

What right have I to sully my family name by living with a man who is not my husband? Have I thought about my mother, my neighbors, my ancestors? And so on. To listen to him, my companion, that poor Italian nightingale, is worse than a terrorist, a drug addict, a spy.

"You know," sneers the Good Cop, "if the Islamists attack you right out in broad daylight, we won't be able to do a thing for you . . ."

The Islamists? That does it. After brandishing the banner of morality and defending the honor of my mother (a woman whose life they permanently destroyed), these two jokers are now insinuating things about my safety and that of the non-Muslim whose presence profanes the holy Islamic soil of Morocco. My patience—which had a few dribbles left, mixed with some crumbs of fear—is at an end.

"I'll fuck whomever I want!"

That lands like a gunshot. Silence falls. Now we can hear

the tape recorder making its faint metallic noise. One of the men clears his throat.

"I'll fuck whomever I want, and if I fuck a foreigner, it's precisely because he isn't a Muslim!"

"You know what they call that?"

"What they call it? Of course I know! And if you don't, I'll enlighten you: it's called fucking a young, handsome Italian actor and a great guy!"

My two interrogators have no time to respond before I rush out onto the balcony, yelling so fast and so uncontrollably that I feel almost possessed by a demon. They took my youth, my name, my life, my father, my identity, my dreams, my sleep, my health, and now they want what I have left, or at least what they think I have left? No! My ass belongs to me, if anything still does. That they will not get, and to prove it, I threaten impulsively to throw myself off the balcony. And at that moment, I think I would almost do so, because I cannot bear the oppression anymore, this cannibal dictatorship that even climbs into bed with those whom it has decided to destroy.

"Okay, okay, calm down," says the Good Cop in a shaky voice, signaling to the others to leave the apartment. Even though I am half hysterical out on my balcony, shaking like a leaf, I know for certain that now *he* is afraid, too—afraid of having to explain to his superiors, who will surely blame him, how his mission went terribly wrong. This is the great paradox of dictatorships: they have given this man the power to terrorize me, to ruin my life, but not to kill me. If I were to decide to take the plunge, the infernal machine would turn on him, his family, his name, and his honor.

"We're going," he repeats three or four times. "Do whatever you want, I wash my hands of the matter."

They leave, with clean hands, and the Italian emerges hesitantly from the bedroom, less masterful than usual.

"Everything's all right?"

Without answering that stupid question, I sit down on the balcony and cry my eyes out.

They've ruined everything, once again.

Antonio stays a few more days, but the honeymoon's over. I can't stand him anymore. He goes home to Naples but telephones me constantly, promising that soon things will run smoothly for what he calls our love, and what I would call our affair. Until the day when he announces ecstatically that he has some wonderful news.

"Malika, I'm giving up everything. Movies, my career, none of that means anything. Give me three weeks, time enough to wrap up my affairs, and I'll come live with you."

"In Morocco?"

"Of course, in Morocco. If you can't leave the country, then I'll come to you!"

Life isn't fair. In an instant, I begin to despise this poor man, who is ready to abandon his career to be with me. I have lived too much in submission to accept it in a man, and now the Italian has just bowed down to the dictatorship. They want to keep me prisoner, deny me a passport, place me under forced residence? Who cares, he will come of his own free will and force himself to live in my residence, to share my life in the shadow of the Commander of the Faithful. Doesn't he understand that I want exactly the opposite? For Prince Charming to rescue the princess from her high tower and carry her off on his white horse, as Eric will?

So now I detest him.

"I don't understand," he moans. "I love you."

There's nothing to understand: we are not made for each other. A few more months of phone calls, mostly his, and it ends, as we both knew it would.

The second sexual experience of my life involves a twenty-two-year-old male model who came to Morocco for a shoot, a handsome specimen completely fabricated in a body-building gym from just the right mix of exercise and health foods. Why did I appeal to him so much? It's a mystery to me. Perhaps he thought the undoubtedly greater experience that went with my age would shoot him straight to cloud nine. If only he'd known what he was getting into, poor boy . . .

The pretty boy does his damnedest to lure me to his hotel room. And no place else, because he has been specifically forbidden to go anywhere near Moroccan women during his short stay in Marrakesh. But Adonis thinks he knows better.

Given his earlier passionate glances and suggestive smiles, I am under no illusion that he wants to play cards with me.

But I am not expecting him to open his door naked as the day he was born.

"Come in."

I *rush* in, terrified at the idea that someone may have seen me, seen *him,* and even more terrified by the realization that this is way beyond Italian songs at sunset. Was I after sex? I think I'm going to get it.

Adonis stretches out languorously on the bed and, reaching over to open the drawer of the night table, pulls out a condom, which he hands to me.

I have absolutely no idea what to do with it.

I struggle with the little packet, not daring to look up. I would give my life to vanish, fly away, disintegrate on the spot. And I am so clumsy that I wind up tearing the condom when I rip open the packet.

I stammer, apologize, get confused. Annoyed, Adonis sits up on the bed and checks the drawer.

"I've only got one left," he grumbles.

Meanwhile, I shut myself up in the bathroom and wash my hands three times to get rid of the slimy stuff on my fingers. Stomach cramps and a pounding headache remind me that much is at stake here, while I try to steady my nerves.

When I return to the arena, doing my best to act like a seductress, my partner hands me the second condom with an amused smile.

"It's the last one—let's not waste it!"

Waste it? Who, me? The idea! I am really careful, so careful that Adonis loses patience, takes back the packet, opens it, and slips the sucker on without my help. And since I just stand there stupidly, he takes my right hand and places it firmly on his penis.

But I am still motionless, clutching his penis like a pilot with a control stick, and wondering what I ought to do with my left hand. Caress his thigh? There's a thought. Or stroke his hair. Adonis is looking at me, and I see in his eyes that he was expecting something else from a woman in her forties. As for me, clamped to his lubricated member, I am empty, vacant, except for my overwhelming shame, doubts, and that headache.

He loosens my grip a little, tries to get my hand going in a movement that I can't follow, then falls back on the bed.

"Not a huge success," he says.

It certainly isn't, as I am the first to know. Adonis will go home to America cursing Arab women, while I am convinced that nothing and no one can help me catch up with my lost life.

A few months later, Eric will come along to prove me wrong. If he is the man of my life, it is not only because I became infatuated with him, like a heroine in a romance novel, or because I have the feeling that I am only half alive when we are apart— those things happen to everyone in love. But Eric knew how to find the key, the golden key that opened my heart and everything else, a key so well hidden that I would have sworn it did not exist. Eric succeeded where all the shrinks failed, and line after line, he rewrote the instruction manual I had thought was lost forever. He did more than make me his wife: he made me a woman.

A providential trip brought Eric to Morocco, where we meet like the most anonymous of free people, during a wedding. He has no way of knowing that this will be for him the beginning of a long and torturous road, an ordeal for which I still reproach myself every day. And I do not know that this tall, strapping fellow with the sly smile, ten years younger than I am, will be my one and only real escape. All I do know is that he does not come on as a seducer or a conqueror, that not for one second do I ever feel threatened in any way. We hardly notice as the hours fly by and our conversation stretches into the early hours of the morning. I can't believe it: I am laughing, and with all my heart. We get along like old friends. He speaks Arabic fluently, having spent his youth in Lebanon. He's sweet, considerate, kind, gentle, smart, funny . . . I'll run out of words before I can finish.

This is the first time since I left prison that an encounter with a man has not ended in panic and disgust. I'm not afraid with him. He's the only one ever to make me feel so safe. All at once I'm sure this man will never bow under pressure or allow anyone to influence him. I feel his strength. I can glimpse his patience and understanding. I know right away that he'll love me for who I really am, and not for anything I might seem. At that moment everything seems so sweet, so natural to me that I could almost simply let myself go, just like that, without thinking about it, forgetting my doubts, my anxieties, my psychological blocks.

I believe in love; tonight, I finally believe. But we are not ready for that yet, unfortunately, and it will take Eric long months of patience and love before this fleeting state of grace comes back to stay. It takes him time to make me his, time he spends willingly. And though even with him I'll have trouble letting myself go, he will always reassure me that it is only a passing phase.

From my touch, from the way I have of speaking to him or sitting down next to him, he understands right away that I am a terrified child dressed up as a woman. He spends our first night together simply holding and caressing me, and I let him. Little by little, without rushing me, he guides me toward what I'd believed impossible: pleasure.

For a year he shuttles between Morocco and France. To stay in closer touch with me, he gives me a cell phone. I'm one of the first people in Casablanca to have one. Even when he's away, I feel protected. Hearing that telephone ring twelve or fifteen times a day makes me feel like the mightiest woman in the world. From now on, there is someone I can count on in my life who will protect me. Before I knew him, I was an orphan, but with him, even when he's not physically at my side, I am someone else: myself. If the word "freedom" has ever really blossomed into meaning for me, it is thanks to him and him alone.

Without ever becoming discouraged, Eric accompanied me through my difficult times on my journey to rejoin society.

When my strength would flag, he would urge me on, tenderly but firmly.

And whenever I would let myself sink into depression and discouragement, when I felt the need to curl up in a corner to wait for life to pass me by, he alone knew how to get me on my feet and back into the fray.

"We'll get there," he would always say, smiling to reassure me.

We. Because there are two of us, and for the first time, I am two. Eric is one of those men who, instead of holding you back, inspire you with the energy you need. I have no great experience with couples, but it seems to me that lasting ones are a rare phenomenon. Eric is simply my other half, a protective and sharing partner. I would follow him to the ends of the world.

It is Eric's first Christmas in Marrakesh. I would like it to be a sexy Christmas, a marathon of loving caresses. We spend long hours in the heart of the medina, in herbalists' shops. I have always enjoyed the company of such people, and one shop owner offers us some interesting traditional stimulants (Viagra has a long ancestry): dwarf tortoises, chameleons, some special West African amulets, or "*gris-gris* for women." While we are at it, I ask him if he might have something for men, too, and the mere fact that I am speaking freely about pleasure gives me great satisfaction. Eric can't get over it: he comes from a country where people think that Moroccan women keep their eyes lowered at all times.

"The Christian: zero?" the guy asks me with a toothless smile.

"No, no, the Christian not zero at all. But I'd like you to give me something so we can party all night long. For him and for me, a little something extra."

He nods. And from the back of his tiny shop he brings out an ancestral recipe whose principal ingredient, he assures me, is powdered hyena. Under Eric's skeptical eye, the herbalist grinds it all up and pours it into a carafe.

"Here you are, my beauty. One teaspoon in a glass of tea for him, and two for you. Or else . . . problems!"

And so, as soon as we return home, the tea ceremony begins. Like a true geisha, I have taken a perfumed bath and slathered myself with lotion. A few drops of musk in the hollow of my throat, with my hair still damp and my peignoir loosely tied, I make a dramatic entrance of which I am not a little proud. It is Eric's last evening in Morocco; tomorrow he is going back to Paris. Thanks to the hyena, if I may put it that way, I know that this evening, and the attendant night, will be unforgettable.

While Eric serves himself a soupspoon of the naughty mixture, I stretch out, my peignoir falling open, offering myself to complete pleasure. A soupspoon . . . The herbalist had said a teaspoon, but what's the difference? Besides, to be sure of not missing out on the mixture's effects, I have already swallowed a spoonful myself when I was alone out in the kitchen, spiking the tea in advance. Too much pleasure can't hurt. Not to mention that one is never too sure of oneself, when there is a whole life to catch up on.

When the man of my life lies down beside me, I feel a little dizzy, and the desire to take a tiny nap overwhelms any erotic impulse. Eric is already snoring when my eyelids close on my plans for a wild night of abandon.

At two in the morning, we wake up without the slightest feeling of desire, except perhaps the desire not to sleep anymore. So Eric will spend his last hours of this Moroccan Christmas in a discothèque, wiggling halfheartedly on the dance floor.

A bleary day is dawning when we huddle together in the taxi taking him to the airport. I am cold, and I feel nauseated. And even with that hyena business behind us, we are depressed by a sense of failure that words cannot dispel. Our last night, even though we know it is not *the* last night, suddenly seems serious to us, and laden with consequences.

The next day, while I am brooding over my despair, the phone rings. It is Eric. Laughing crazily.

"Guess what?"

"What?"

"I have a nonstop hard-on! It started on the plane, and ever since—it's hopeless! I am permanently stuck in the upright position."

Eric did not lay down his weapon, so to speak, for three days. From the depths of his Parisian solitude, he must have cursed me, me and every quack in the medina, with their powders, their amulets, their infusions, and their miracle ointments. I still have trouble imagining how a half-open peignoir would have been enough on its own to make me desirable, but the hyena powder has been banished to the bottom of a cupboard, next to some disgusting peanut butter someone once brought me.

A few months later, our love finally emerges into the full light of day, in France. I live with him. Every night I sleep by his side. Every morning he leaves for work, the better to come home to me every evening.

An established, cherished, delightfully legitimate sexuality now replaces those weekends stolen from the surveillance and the disapproval of others. But Eric's ordeal is not yet over. Frustrated, stifled, repressed for so long, the phantasm of motherhood returns with a vengeance, slipping between us and our pleasure. There is nothing else but that searing idea: to have a child. To become a mother.

Mama . . . the sweetest word of all the words I know. In all the languages of the world, it means the same thing: the love between a woman and her child.

To make it mine, I will push open every door for three years: I, who cannot order an omelet without feeling faint, I schedule test after test.

I want a child. I want others to consider me a mother, to talk to me about my kid, to bore me to tears with idiotic questions: What class is he in, has he cut his teeth yet, wherever did you get that cute anorak? I want to enter the extremely exclusive club of billions of doting mothers whose universe is reduced to Junior's latest exploits. He said "Papa," he pointed at the moon, he offered me a necklace of noodles. And if he is a girl, she will want a princess dress and the magic wand that goes with it.

Sex becomes rational, scientific. We count the days, the cycles, the highs and the lows. I begin asking myself painful questions about the validity of being a couple, of sex, of this pleasure that we take where others are procreating.

I no longer know what is right, what is true. All this might almost make me hate the man of my life, whom I love more than everything.

An Italian with a Nazi attitude whom I had met on a film set a few years earlier, an amateur Göring complete with boots and a whip, once told me something I have never forgotten: "You and your sisters, your duty in life is to bear children."

I cannot forget those words. It does not matter whether the fellow was nostalgic for the glory days of the Blackshirts or not: I often tell myself that he was right.

Eric lives through all this without falling apart, without losing hope, and above all without abandoning his battle to make of me, almost against my will, a free woman.

For our wedding night, he reserves a sumptuous suite at the Hôtel Raphaël, a magical place, the kind all girls dream of—

whatever their age. A peach-colored negligee (which matches the room décor) is spread out on the bed like a ravishing promise. A magnum of champagne, chocolates, the curtains drawn, soft lights—everything is ready for the main event in a fairy-tale setting . . . where all our friends will camp out until five in the morning.

Because at seven on the dot, Eric has an appointment at the clinic to masturbate, to deposit in a little tube the precious semen that we hope will make me a mother.

A pile of porn magazines at seven in the morning, on the day after your wedding night . . .

"I hate you," he tells me, still wearing that smile I can never resist. "This is the worst wedding night in history!"

I think I've married a saint.

15
MOURNING

The telephone is ringing, ringing, and at last I wake up. It is July 23, 1999, and I have no idea that my wounds are all suddenly about to be reopened. I pick up the phone and recognize the voice of a Moroccan friend, calling me from Casablanca in the utmost secrecy, because it is not good for those still in the country to be caught communicating with my family.

"*He* is dead," she whispers.

Dead! My throat tightens, and it takes me a few seconds to breathe freely again.

"Did you hear me?"

"Yes, I heard you."

There is no need to ask her whom she means. I know. "The one whose name must not be spoken" is not Allah, but that man, Hassan II, King of Morocco, whose shadow has weighed for so long on the country that we all thought he was immortal. The Ogre has just proved that the powerful must die like everyone else, and that power, even absolute power, cannot save you. Still, after I have hung up, I can't manage to believe it. The statue of the commander, so strongly bolted to its pedestal, seems to me—and to all of us—forever indestructible. For a lifetime, I have centered all my doubts, my questions, my sorrow, and my hatred on that statue. Can it disappear from the surface of the earth because of a simple phone call?

I need to confirm the news, make it official, see it, hear it. All the TV stations have picked up on the story, broadcasting short reviews of his reign, showing images from their film archives: Hassan II in his youth, Hassan II getting older, Hassan II in his old age. We see him everywhere, on foot, in a car, waving to the crowd, on a balcony, at official functions, traveling. So many handshakes, so many fixed and diplomatic smiles, for the West, the East, the Middle East. Watching them parade by in their film clips, you would think that every head of state in the twentieth century had lined up to have a family picture taken with the King of Morocco. Hassan II is not even cold yet and already he is history. The commentaries buzzing in my ears overflow with praise for this great man, for whom every journalist mourns as for a father, in a voice strangled by on-air emotion.

As of seven o'clock the next morning, every media outlet in the Francophone world is camped out on my doorstep, to

Eric's deep despair, as he had hoped to have a quiet lunch at L'Entrecôte on this sunny July day.

"They're downstairs," he tells me with a rueful smile.

They are indeed. They are from every French TV channel, Belgian TV, plus the cable and radio stations, along with a few curious onlookers, drawn to the cameras like moths to a light. They pepper me with questions. The same ones, always the same ones.

"What are you feeling?"

What am I feeling? I don't even know myself. Great anxiety regarding the transfer of power, the future of Morocco, the fate of my friends who still live there. But that is not what the journalists have come to hear. My tormentor is dead, and they have come to see me jump for joy, pop champagne corks, dance a jig in the lobby of my building, caught in their lights. Images they would circulate with the caption, "Oufkir: a second liberation," or something like that. And when I show no kind of satisfaction—I feel only a vague emptiness, so how could I display any joy?—they try to make me say what they would like to hear.

"It must be such a relief for you!"

"Do you feel better now?"

No, it is not a relief, and no, I do not feel better. Twenty years of my life vanished into the belly of the Ogre, and his death will not give me back my youth. Or my father. The executioner died a good death, in his own bed, with all his honors, and every TV and radio station in the world is paying homage to him this morning.

Calmly, I explain that my thoughts today are only of Morocco, that I am neither happy nor unhappy at the death of Hassan II, that I hope the country will weather this trial without mishap. But no one wants to listen to me.

"Still, it must have been something of a shock to hear the news."

"A bit of a shock, yes."

"And it's a kind of revenge, after all, no?"

"No, absolutely not."

They look so frustrated that I feel like adding, "Sorry!"

Packing up their cameras, the journalists leave empty-handed, with neither tears nor laughter "in the can," nothing to cause a sensation on the eight o'clock news.

They are so disappointed that they will now edit things to support their claim that instead of rejoicing, I am mourning the death of the King. Because for the media, you are either happy or unhappy, and there are no gray areas in between. I read in the newspapers that I was trying to curry favor with the new regime (go figure that one) by making a show of genuine grief. One reporter bolder than the rest even launched into a brilliant psychological analysis in which he proved, by adding A to B, that I was suffering from Stockholm syndrome and was a victim in love with my torturer.

I would doubtless have been overjoyed if Hassan II had admitted his crimes before he died, if my family's name had been publicly cleared, and if the butcher's public image had been tarnished by the cruelties of his regime. But he takes his leave embalmed on a catafalque, in an odor of incense and an atmosphere of servility, as everyone jostles to be seen in a good position, striving to be the one who loved him the most, knew him the best, served him the most loyally. "This great friend of France," "this great democrat," intone the politicians, who certainly hope that his successor will be as well disposed toward them as his father was.

Hassan II leaves me orphaned, bereft of my pain: his death deprives me of my reason to hate, to fight, to suffer, and it was that pain that kept me going all those years in prison. As the hours pass, I feel a deep and growing sadness, for the Ogre's death is in a small way my own. Gone forever without settling his accounts, he takes into the grave my last chance of understanding. Why? I would have liked so much for him to have one day answered in person the question that has haunted me for so many years. Why? Why us? Why me, who was almost his daughter?

I will never hear the answer to my questions. And with that final amputation, stripping me once again of my identity—my identity as victim—Hassan II leaves the stage forever, still with the upper hand. And the tiny moment of death, which comes for us all and has claimed him at last, cannot change a thing about that.

"Naturally, you are opposed to the monarchy," a reporter says, hoping that I will at least rail against the system, even if I refuse to dance on the King's grave.

Fresh disappointment: he learns that I support the principle of a monarchist regime, because I know how necessary it is to the unity of my country. To my mind, Hassan II is no longer either father or torturer; he is a faceless public figure who leaves behind a fragile nation threatened by all the excesses of an Arab world in crisis. I am not imbued with the Muslim principle that forbids any criticism of the dead, but I cannot say that the Ogre who ruled Morocco for forty years did nothing but harm to the country. If only Mohammed VI could prove less bloodthirsty, and consign his father's despotic behavior to the nightmares of the past, the regime he has inherited might turn out to be the best one possible.

"I understand," says the reporter, who understands most of all that he will have to go elsewhere to feed his voyeurism. I never saw a peep of that interview anywhere in the press.

That is the second time I have disappointed the media, and they will be irritated enough to invent their own interpretations of how I feel. My tormentor's death is like my arrival in Paris: these two major changes in my life were not occasions of great joy, or even relief. Relief came later, gradually, when I began to write. Paper absorbs my memories and my words, removing their heavy burden from my shoulders at last. It was not major events that released me from this weight, but writing.

FREEDOM

For the moment, and while a world in mourning prepares to give Hassan II the funeral rites my father never had, I expect much from the new regime. A word, one word would be enough. But a king is not required to confess; these are things expected of mere mortals, those whom one throws into prison. A king, like an assassin, recognizes no justice but his own.

As for the people, they are not inclined to forget, and that is what has given me the strength to keep hoping after so many years. When I was released in 1991, policemen would salute me respectfully at every red light. How ironic it was to see men formerly assigned to our guard detail approach me in broad daylight to assure me of their unconditional sympathy and admiration for my father.

Throughout the city, the forces of order would blow their whistles, stopping traffic to let me pass. My country is undoubtedly the only one where, fresh out of prison, one may ignore the traffic lights with the blessings of the police and sail through intersections like a VIP. Of course, these men respected the *Mahzen,* the conservative system that rules Morocco and meticulously defines the divine power of the King and his servants, and they would not speak ill of the regime. But they paid their respects to the memory of my father, executed by the sovereign they served.

Strangely enough, the only revenge, the only satisfaction I will gain from the death of Hassan II, will come from an entirely unexpected quarter: the press. The worst thing that can happen to a statesman is not when people speak harshly of him, but when they do not speak of him at all. And Moroccans know better than anyone how to use a healthy form of amnesia: barely a few weeks after the death of the great man, there was hardly a mention of him in the press. He may belong to history, but before the official mourning period was over, he was already yesterday's news, no longer of any interest to the newspapers from which his face had almost disappeared.

The country's major daily paper—which was the government's voice while the King was alive—finally dares to publish a front-page article reexamining the affair that bears my name. The Palace issues no confession, makes no excuses, but shaking off its fear at last, for the first time in twenty-seven years the press does not hesitate to print the cursed name of my family. And for the first time, I see my father's picture spread out over the front page, while down in a corner, modest and almost unnoticeable, the King's photo is so small you have to bring it up to your nose to recognize him.

16
AMERICAN DREAMS

When I was seventeen and wore truly scary mini-skirts, the United States stood for everything I'd ever dreamed of. It's hard to believe I was ever that girl, but the least you could say is that I knew how to have fun. Before facing the unpleasant prospect of my baccalauréat exam, I snuck off to New York, as I would later to Paris, Rabat, and Casablanca. In New York I befriended Marvin Dayan, the nephew of Moshe Dayan, the Israeli defense minister, which gave the King's ministers fits. My father simply smiled. Back then, I could go out every night, as blissfully oblivious of danger as I was of my own charms.

In Los Angeles, I accompanied Princess Nehza, the youngest sister of Hassan II, and we were welcomed by all of Hollywood. I met world-famous movie stars: Zsa Zsa Gabor, Edward G. Robinson—Steve McQueen even gave me a ride in his dune buggy in Malibu. How far away it all seems now! To think

I might have become an actress with a few divorces under her belt, sunning herself beside an azure swimming pool in Hollywood . . .

The United States no longer fascinates the rest of the world so much, perhaps because that world has gotten smaller, and planes fly faster, and you don't need to shout into the telephone to be heard in New York. For me, however, nothing has changed. And even though my first book has been published in many European countries, it's hard for me to believe my editor, who assures me that with any luck, my story will soon be available "in the U.S." My book, in America? Impossible, unthinkable. I have already had trouble grasping the fact that I am being read in Europe, that people are interested in me, and many people, too, if I am to believe the figures I am sent every week, as if I were selling nickel on the commodities exchange. But America, that's too much. Much too much.

"It's quite simple," explains my editor with a smile. "If someone has to go sell your book in the U.S., well then, you will go to the U.S. It will only be published if you go promote it over there. Americans don't buy things by correspondence; they want to feel the merchandise."

"They are not going to be feeling anything at all," I reply, terrified. "My going there is out of the question."

"You do this to me over every book signing, Malika."

"This time, it's different. I can't. I won't go."

Three days later, I am on the plane, my head buzzing with all the advice people give to little girls who travel alone. Don't forget your passport. Keep your boarding pass with you. Take your fur-lined jacket; it's cold in New York.

I keep going over the images I had of America when I was seventeen, but they do not comfort me, because the carefree young princess of those days is dead and buried, along with glittering soirées like the dinner parties at Zsa Zsa Gabor's house, where my father felt right at home with his relaxed charm. Today those memories seem so distant that they might as well belong to someone else, like a sepia photograph found in an attic.

New York: clutching my passport, I cross that famous yellow line behind which so many immigrants have dreamed of their new lives. Then everything happens quickly: a publicist and a chauffeur arrive to pick me up, while my luggage, claimed by invisible hands, finds its way into the limousine's trunk. Welcome to America, they tell me, calling me by my first name. Did I have a good trip? Yes, thank you. The waiting line for taxis seems endless, but who cares, our car is parked right outside the exit, with all its lights blinking. I sink into the soft back seat. They offer me a glass of Perrier straight from a mini-bar gleaming with neon. The limo does not roll along the expressway, it glides, and the lights stream past so quickly that I see only streaks of color.

The publicist is already explaining the schedule that lies ahead of me, bombarding me with information: the name of my hotel, the current weather, the strategies to follow if I want to make a first-class media splash. The chauffeur says nothing, however; that's normal, he is a chauffeur, and in the rearview mirror I can see his eyes fixed on the road ahead. And who am I, that he should be driving me like a servant, without ever meeting my eyes in that mirror? Even though I was waited on all through my childhood, I no longer have the heart for it, and I feel a pang of guilt at the thought that he is there to serve me. It bothers me, and I would almost like to apologize to him. This evening, those press conferences in Lyon or Strasbourg seem so far away, and those arrivals by train when, often alone, I had to find a taxi to drop me off at a little rural hotel of outdated charm. At this moment in the limousine, America is truly that familiar figment of my imagination, a terrifying yet entrancing machine that has swooped down and carried me off toward a future all laid out before me. I close my eyes, hypnotized by the purring of the engine. This evening I am being treated like a star, a VIP, as they say in the free world. All this for a book, my book, a simple account of a woman's life in prison?

"It's perfectly normal for us to welcome you," smiles the woman sitting beside me. "We're very happy to have you here. I'll be by to pick you up in a little while, after you've had a chance to freshen up a bit."

We are already at the hotel, where a valet in green opens the door for me, while another places my luggage on a large golden trolley. And once more, Welcome, Good evening, madame. I am directed toward a huge counter where a concierge so spruce and trim he could be the Prince of Wales has me sign a form. Everything is moving too quickly, I'm having trouble keeping up. The hotel lobby is dizzyingly vast, all in marble and mirrors. So many people are hurrying through it that it almost seems like some kind of luxurious train station concourse. After my passport vanishes (for once, I have no time to worry about it), I receive a sort of credit card I am informed is my key, and another little man in green leads me off, with my golden chariot, toward the four elevators, also gleaming with gold. "Ding" goes the first one, upholstered in leather with mahogany trim, just like a limousine. The valet delivers me and my luggage to the room, then wishes me a pleasant stay. America is the land where they wish you the most good things. A good time, a good trip, a good visit, good afternoon, good evening . . . If a mere fraction of these wishes comes true, the United States must really be a paradise on earth.

"Where is the TV remote?" I ask the valet nervously.

"Here, madame."

"Ah."

The fellow knows his job, and realizing that I am a bit uncertain about how the remote works (it took me more than a month to master the subtleties of the one in Paris), he undertakes to explain it to me. Press here, to change the channel; there, for the satellite menu (satellite? I am in the world of James Bond!); the volume control is below, the on-off button is on top, the rest doesn't matter.

And the heat and air conditioning? A huge dial stuck in the wall, with notches and numbers everywhere. And the coffeepot? No, I do not know how to use that, either. Patiently, the valet explains that, too. And more. Still smiling, he will spend at least forty-five minutes going over the sink (go figure how to use that big mushroom you turn and pull in every direction until you get the right temperature), the mini-bar (locked, no doubt to keep me from stealing anything), the six light switches accessible from the bed, and the small safe hanging from the clothes rod in the closet (a closet you could easily rent out to a couple of students).

I am so afraid of forgetting some secret of this technological laboratory that I call the unfortunate valet back ten times, just when he has almost reached the elevator. As for giving him a tip, I think about it, but I am afraid of offending him. How much? And how do I do it? Discreetly, with a smile? Do I just hold out a bill? If I were he, I would hate that. One dollar, ten dollars: too little, too much—I have no way of knowing, and when I finally decide on a course of action, whether I am right or not hardly matters, because he is long gone.

Luckily I have the TV, familiar and reassuring, aside from the fact that it insists on speaking English. There are hundreds of channels, way too many for a single pair of eyes, and more than enough for the most blasé customer. Who cares about the program—the little screen is my friend, my American friend, available and devoted, day and night. For two days, aside from the times when the publicist arrives to stuff me into a limousine, I will watch TV without leaving my room. Outside is New

York, the enormous, legendary city that makes Paris look like a sleepy little town. It took me months to brave tiptoeing around Paris, supported by the man of my life and my friends. So nothing on earth will make me explore the Big Apple on my own and wander through the tall columns of steam shooting up into the icy air from the manhole covers in the middle of the street. New York seems to be breathing under my feet and might swallow me down in one gulp.

Finally, the real book promotion begins. I can't believe my eyes. And I thought I'd seen it all by now!

"We'll be presenting you to all the interested TV stations," I learn at my first meeting with my American publisher.

Compared with the American media juggernaut, Parisian book promotion (which I had thought worthy of a Michael Jackson tour) is just a stroll in the countryside. New York is a kettle of boiling-hot water, and I am plunged right in as if I were a tea bag. My first lunch with CBS made me positively dizzy; I had to eat, have a conversation, know all the answers, and do it all in English! And then *60 Minutes,* CNN—the big guns, the publicity department tells me joyfully, while my limo races around nonstop. Unwilling to lose an instant, the publicist takes advantage of traffic jams to work the phones, the one in the car as well as her cell. God gave publicity people two ears, for which they give thanks every day.

"Hold on a second . . ."

And she checks her agenda, crossing out, erasing, turning pages feverishly, at least when her "organizer" is not in play. The organizer is a sort of all-knowing instrument as big as a cigarette pack that you poke with a tiny stylus to make it talk. I almost feel sorry for it, this thing they have tried ten times to explain to me and that they torture mercilessly like Gestapo agents. They stab at it, again and again, and the organizer finally spills the beans, coughing up everything: names, numbers, dates, and times. Supposedly, you can stash the contents of an entire dictionary in one of those things. Even better: it corrects your spelling, like a tiny teacher, as you tap at the keys. I long ago gave up trying to decipher these cryptic mysteries; all I care about now is resting for a few moments before the limo stops again someplace where I will be hustled outside, welcomed, and thrown back into the whirlwind.

Oh, America! I've never stopped roaming this enormous land. Everything here is supersized. Steaks so big they just need hoofs to be cows again, potatoes by the shovelful, and even though people keep saying that American food is not as good as the cream of French gastronomy, to me it looks like a burst of generosity. Instead of galantines or puff pastries on the menu, there are astronomical amounts of food, which have given rise to the system of the doggy bag. This invention definitely does not go to the dogs, however, and Eric explains to me that the expression dates back to when people worried about saving appearances. Instead, the doggy bag allows Americans to do freely what I do secretly: stockpile food.

Socially acceptable stockpiling frees me from my Parisian shame: here I no longer have to hide what I am doing, and I brazenly collect doggy bags that begin to pile up at my hotels. I do not eat my hoarded leftovers at home in Paris, and I will not be eating these pizza crusts, pieces of steak, or cold potatoes, either, but I know that they are there.

And while I am at it, I also pounce on those tiny products with the hotel logos—the lotions, shampoos, cotton swabs, small bars of soap—that unseen hands set out every day in hotel bathrooms. It's just that they are so cute, like doll accessories. Only in America would such luxury be offered to everybody and be renewed daily without costing you extra. Soon I have to buy a second travel bag, which fills up with these inexhaustible treasures. Won't Eric be pleased!

What will please him most of all is the astounding way in which my story has seized the spotlight, allowing me to exorcise the last of my demons. The book is a success, people tell me so every day, and I have even signed autographs out in the street, as if every passerby were now familiar with my life. That's it—my revenge, my victory: telling the whole world, right in the face of Hassan II, about the horror he inflicted on my family and thousands of others. The silence is broken. First France, then French-speaking countries, and now all-powerful America have listened to the cry that resurrects my father's name. My name. And what can he do about it, this omnipotent monarch, capable of sending an entire family into a hellish dungeon with a snap of his fingers? Nothing. Not even a little execution, a small, casual arrest. Nothing. He can only listen to my voice, coming from all directions, and wherever he is, I hope he's sorry now.

Now and then, our little publicity crew finds itself in the eye of the hurricane, where my companions take the time to touch base with one another while they are dispatching their club sandwiches. Did anyone send the book to Oprah? Yes, but they have not had a call back. In spite of one or two follow-ups.

"Try her again," the publisher says between two mouthfuls of sandwich, his ear glued to the phone.

I choose that moment to voice an opinion, for perhaps the first time since I have been tossed into this tempest. Because it is a little painful, this silent submission that must make me seem like a fool to them.

"Call her back—a third time? Who does this woman think she is?"

Three heads swivel toward me, as though I had insulted God the Father.

"Oprah Winfrey!"

"Oh, of course."

I say "of course," but I have absolutely no idea who Oprah Winfrey is. Not a clue in the world. My companions are vastly amused, so I can guess that she is definitely someone. I can't even imagine yet how much she is someone, in every sense of the word, and how much our meeting will change my life.

And we might just as easily never have met. During my grueling publicity marathon in 2001, Tina Brown, then head of Talk Miramax, threw a lunch for fortysome influential women. My friend Natalie Marciano told me that lots of powerful media mavens would be there, and that Oprah might show up.

"So what?" I'd said. "Who's she?" Actually, she wasn't there, but one of her producers was, and my story interested her.

Then another opportunity appeared. Tina took me to a vast hall occupied by a minimum of 2,000 people, drowning in the deafening noise; I felt like a strange creature being exhibited for the civilized white man. I'm introduced to and embraced by strangers full of superficial empathy. Staggering toward the buffet, I glimpse a brawny woman, an earpiece informing her of my every movement, who gives me a thumbs-up: "Nice job on *60 Minutes*!" A few minutes later, the lady bodyguard approachs me and asks me politely to follow her to the VIP lounge.

Why not?

At the end of my tether, I throw myself on an immaculate white sofa unoccupied by a single soul. I learn that it's reserved for Oprah. I bolt upright, as if from an electric shock, and try to head back toward the crowd. And then there she is: Oprah. She studies me, draws closer, and announces with a determined air: "Tomorrow I'm going to read your book." She takes me in her arms and then, more affectionately, as though sharing an intimate secret, vows, "I promise."

In the plane on the way back to Paris, I can't stop thinking about this land where anything is possible, where neither menopause nor sterility nor prison could prevent me from starting over. Why not?

But my day-to-day life lies far away from all this. It lies, to be precise, at home, where I've just made Eric some cutlets in mushroom cream sauce with pasta. It's ten at night when the phone rings. Oh, no. A soft voice is speaking in English on the other end. Oprah is asking me to return to the States to be a guest on her show in May 2001. She's just chosen my book for her club, and for the first time in her career, she is asking an author to participate in her show. I will have to answer questions from a panel of women selected from among 4,000 applicants.

What happened next belongs to the annals of publishing: Miramax Books, my American publisher, will sell hundreds of thousands of copies. But even this success was nothing compared to the emotions that reigned onstage during Oprah's show on that momentous day in May. You had to be there. Perhaps you were . . .

Laden with bags and souvenirs, I head back to Paris again, where the man I miss more and more each day is waiting for me. I am wiped out, relieved, dazed, and happy. As I board the plane, I feel a slight pang at the idea that a small part of me will remain here in America, because it is still the land of exiles, of travelers without a country. I, too, am descended from those who came over on the *Mayflower*, or joined the Exodus, or sailed on those lost ships full of souls in pain and eager to begin again. I have no more roots, and if the earth of Europe is too hard for those who would like to plant themselves there, the soil of America is more welcoming, almost perfectly prepared for anyone who wishes to flourish here. I can't stay in Paris.

A pilgrim once more, I return to the New World, headed this time for Miami. More than in Los Angeles, where I have many friends, I feel that in this city bursting with Hispanic flavor, crisscrossed by the paths of all sorts of immigrants, starting over again is truly possible. I get along well on my own here; even driving seems easier to me. Eric helps Nawal and me settle in. Cleansed of my past, almost a blank slate, I begin working away in a bookstore café on the very book you're reading right now. Eric joined me for good a year later. I now divide my time between Miami and Marrakesh.

17
REBORN

For several days now, Tazmamart has existed. Officially. All around me, whole families are breathing again, clearing a fearful silence from their lungs. Tazmamart, that death camp where so many political prisoners "disappeared," that underworld lost out in mid-desert, that prison the Ogre's administration called a collective hallucination—Tazmamart exists today as if it had appeared on the map with a wave of a magic wand. And now, after so many years of endless mourning by the families of those who never returned, I am grateful to Mohammed VI, who has admitted the inadmissible. The unthinkable. Yes, they sent hundreds of political prisoners there, including the soldiers of the failed coup d'état of 1972, soldiers loyal to my father. Only twenty-seven survived. What happened to the others? Night and Fog, Himmler would have replied. Vanished, gone up in smoke. Who knows why.

With tears in my eyes, I follow the long column of 4×4s

that are finally allowed access to the outskirts of the camp. There, a few hundred meters from the place where their fathers, husbands, brothers disappeared forever into the sand, my friends give themselves up to a grief that for the first time is not tinged with anger. How many are here? Dozens, hundreds: the victims' families, the humanitarian associations, and the press all form one single body, one mass of sorrow. Finally, the long uncertainty is over: the fight for recognition is finished, and now the healing can begin.

Tazmamart exists, Ben Barka's son has come back to the country with his family, and Serfaty has returned from exile.* Two pilots who survived the death camp have written books about the appalling ordeal, published in Morocco. (*Operation Borag F5: The Attack on the Royal Boeing* by Ahmad El Ouafi, the chief of technical resources at Kenitra's air base, and *Kabazal: Walled Up Alive* by Salah Hachad, second commander of Ken-

---

* Mehdi Ben Barka, a gifted mathematician, was a founder of the Union Nationale des Forces Populaires and a leader in the movement to oust the French from Morocco. His radical politics and economic development programs made him a leader of the Moroccan opposition to the regimes of King Mohammed V and his successor, Hassan II. On October 29, 1965, Ben Barka was kidnapped outside the Brasserie Lipp in Paris by two French police officers and was never seen again. General Oufkir, then Minister of the Interior, was one of the people accused by the French of arranging the murder of Ben Barka, for which crime he was sentenced in absentia to life imprisonment.

Abraham Serfaty, a radical student and union leader in the 1960s, shared Ben Barka's dream of a free and open Morocco. Accused of seeking to overthrow the monarchy and establish a republic, he spent seventeen years in jail, after which King Hassan II stripped him of his Moroccan nationality and exiled him to France, where he remained for eight years.

After the death of Hassan II, King Mohammed VI gave Mr. Serfaty and the exiled family of Mehdi Ben Barka permission to return to Morocco. [Translator's note] itra's air base.) The truth gradually pries the cover off a coffin laden with forty years of tyranny. Only one episode remains desperately concealed: for reasons I cannot understand, the "Oufkir affair" is still shrouded in official silence. My book, *Stolen Lives,* is still banned in Morocco. Royal despotism refuses, now and forever, to allow my family the right to be acknowledged as victims. For how much longer? A lifetime, perhaps. It seems that I will pay endlessly for a crime I did not commit. But it does not matter: my sweetest revenge is this new life that no one may take back from me. Although this new existence may be painful at times, with every passing day I draw closer to the daily life of those who live in freedom, because I am, simply, free. And I am beginning a third life, as a woman just like any other (or almost), in a world that will one day become mine. After all, when you have made your home in a king's palace, and then in the blackest of jails, you ought to be able to get used to anything. As I write these lines, I have even learned how to spot my favorite yogurt, nestling among its myriad look-alikes. Fat-free black cherry. With real fruit.

But you cannot tame a hostile universe all by yourself. The man of my life rescued me from hell; two women taught me to live again—two women both alike and different, to whom I owe the small glow of serenity that gleams brighter within me from day to day.

The first one, Helen Bamber, had seen other prisoners

before me: in 1945, when she was nineteen years old, this extraordinary woman went into the recently opened concentration camps to help bring back to life those who had thought they were dead. She took care of them and listened to them. Ever since, without losing her youthful passion and goodness, without growing bitter or disillusioned, she has fought human tragedy on every front, wherever bruised bodies and souls need her.

She is the one who has taught me to accept the hatred and rebellion that I was repressing in myself, who taught me to let out my first cry, a primal cry without which I would no doubt have remained beaten down for the rest of my days. It is Helen who taught me to express out loud that stifled rage, the fearful hatred, all those things you try to hold in to avoid becoming worse than your torturers. It was then that I saw clearly how those cramped and silenced feelings turn into an acid that eats away at the fragile foundations on which I still depend.

For years, people said of me with admiration, "It's amazing. She doesn't hate anyone!"

And I turned the other cheek, encouraged by those who praised me as the Mother Teresa of dictatorship. What they did not know, and what I myself did not realize, was that the resentment I refused to express was stewing somewhere deep inside me, disguised by my attempts to speak only words of conciliation. I have learned from Helen Bamber, however, that peace can be attained only after one has settled one's own accounts. Trapped by my self-image as a prisoner, unable to express the slightest violent emotion, I was playing my role as a victim to grim perfection.

"Come out of yourself; cast off this skin that isn't yours!"

Helen was right. Once you spit out hatred, it weakens and evaporates, leaving you able to breathe again, free to love or to hate not on principle, but by choice.

My parents abandoned me: it has taken all this time for me to admit it. With Helen's help, I have cut the umbilical cord.

My second benefactress is Oprah Winfrey, whose first name alone is enough to open any door in the United States (hit TV programs are like an almost magical "Open, Sesame!" throughout the world of freedom). We first met in the glittering universe of showbiz, a shark-infested realm where she manages to be completely at home. Oprah, however, is the perfect opposite of her peers: in a way, she is the one percent of humanity the major channels grudgingly exempt from their overwhelming devotion to profit. She gives the middle class a voice and offers the victims of horror and injustice a chance to speak out. Others have done this before her, of course, and not always for altruistic motives. I have seen countless programs on which misfortune was fed to the vile appetites of voyeurs. Tearful widowers, drug addicts on the verge of overdose, mugging victims, gang-war survivors, deceived husbands, victims of judicial errors, run-over dogs . . . Television has plenty of everything, especially misery.

But Oprah is not mired in complacency like so many others. Helen Bamber taught me that I had a right to rebel;

227

it was Oprah who taught me about the right to be happy. Because she was the one who best realized how "victimized" my personality was, and she was the one who challenged the fate that was preventing me from reaching for happiness.

"That fate doesn't exist," she kept saying. "You're the one who created it."

Could this be the last stage of my rebirth? Happiness is the last goal, and it is so hard for me to convince myself to strive for it. At the end of my interview with her back in 2001, Oprah said something that I still remember every day.

"Tell me that you can be happy."

Carried away by my emotions and Oprah's charm, feeling pressured by the media spotlight, I replied, "Yes." To great applause. Without thinking about it, without believing it. Or perhaps I did believe it at the time . . . Today, I do not know if I can be happy. Time will tell, of course, unless I pass right by happiness without seeing it. I am a bit like that aging actor who played Dracula for twenty years: consumed by his role, he slept every evening in his coffin and was finally buried in his mauve-lined black cape. I may not have fangs, but my role as a victim is like a second nature to me, and I fear I may never be completely free of it. Will I be buried in my prisoner's skin? The two women who assisted me toward my rebirth have assured me otherwise. Helen gave me the strength to fight back, while Oprah urged me to ask myself the most important question of all. I do not know what my capacity for happiness is, but for them, I will do my best.

I watch Oprah every day with the strange feeling that she is speaking to me, and to me alone. This ritual, which sometimes makes Eric smile, gives me the encouragement I need to seek the happiness I miss so much. I feel as though I am recharging my batteries, absorbing my friend's positive energy. We do not talk with each other often, just a phone call now and then, but her show is like a visit with her. That's all I need to make me happy. And millions of people who have never known either horror or prison seek happiness without any guarantee of success (let's hope there is enough to go around).

By writing this sequel to *Stolen Lives*, I know that I'm freeing myself from misfortune and unhappiness. For better or for worse, I'm becoming a normal person. But that's not all. As you know by now, I like to step from the shadows and make myself heard.

18
REPARATIONS

Money doesn't heal anything. And yet the world tries, with dollars, euros, and dirhams, to dress the wounds of those it has hurt. Whatever it is—a judicial blunder, a defective coffeepot that explodes and disfigures you, twenty years in a penal colony for having been the daughter of the wrong man—a check will make it better. People in the free world worship money so much that they end up quite sincerely believing that it can cure all ills. I've often wondered how people calculate the exact cost of injuries . . . How much for a year in a hospital, a month in prison, a missing leg, or a loved one run over by a bus? At the whims of nations and lawyers, a price is put on everything. Plaintiff and defendant are locked in a grudge match, the former trying to pump the latter for all he's worth, the latter doing his best to cling to every cent. The funniest part is that those who win the best compensation aren't always those who have suffered the most—they just have the best lawyers, for the best lawyers, like the best yogurts, are the most expensive. The poorest litigants, who get their lawyers at rock-bottom prices, will be poorly compensated at the hour of redress.

In 1999, after I had long since given up hope of ever seeing the Moroccan government confess its part in my family's persecution, a committee was created with a charter to compensate the victims of tyranny or, more precisely, to offer financial reparation to those who had paid dearly for the many "judicial" errors of the Commander of the Faithful. Better late than never. In this way my name appeared for the first time on a list of victims. That I could lay claim to compensation implied there had been an offense; this was the sole apology, grudgingly muttered, that I would ever get from Morocco for having taken twenty years of my life. It wasn't much, but it was already enormous, even if I had to wait until 2005 for the announcement that my damages had been "assessed" and a figure assigned: I was finally an officially recognized victim.

This recognition, in the end, persuaded me to accept their nominal sum. Not without reluctance, for if it lifted the final barrier between myself and freedom, it also absolved my tormentors of their responsibility at a bargain price. To accept the government's money was in a way to say that accounts had been settled between the Ogre and me. There was no mistaking the hint of contempt in the eyes of the bureaucratic clerk who stiffly and silently handed me the check. Something in his look seemed to say: here, take your money and get out. Suddenly I felt like an alms collector. One hand out to take the check, I was a beggar who should thank him for his charity. We'd swapped roles; I was indebted to my tormentors. My suffering had been bought and never again would I have the right to protest.

If my friends hadn't convinced me otherwise, I would have flung the check right back in that clerk's mocking face, to prove to the world that mere money, and not a single acknowledgment or apology, was no way to redeem suffering. But I hadn't forgotten the advice of those who loved me. Refuse the reparations? Out of the question! My tormentors had no pride, and my own would have fallen flat. The government would simply have been spared the expense of compensating me, that's all.

"You don't want their money?" my friends exclaimed. "They'll be thrilled!"

Saving money always brings satisfaction to people in the free world.

Yet my check was hardly a fortune. A fraction, really, of what someone might wrest from McDonald's for having burned his tongue on coffee served too hot. A committee whose members were 100 percent Moroccan—and that was all I knew about them—had rather arbitrarily come up with a figure after taking into account this and that: age, gender, whatever. Despite the twenty years we'd all lost, my mother, brothers, and sisters were awarded different amounts in damages. I didn't care; the money would serve to put this free woman back in debt for fifteen years by fulfilling my dream of buying a house all my own and no one else's. A place to call home, a cocoon, a lair. How ironic that my imprisonment should one day be transformed into my first real home!

Nothing can make up for twenty years, or ten years, or even six months of jail, least of all this little check or the house it bought me. It wouldn't have made a difference had it been for a million dollars. The amount was irrelevant to the wild elation that followed. Although nothing can erase suffering, my tormentors had finally acknowledged, before the entire world, what my family had gone through. My name had been cleared, and that was priceless.

All it took to become a rich woman was a signature on a piece of paper. And if my wealth remains relative, I might as well have been the Queen of England to the ragged man who approached me as I left the court. He wasn't a beggar, he explained, but a chef. Life had not been kind to him, for in a few days he was to be operated on for advanced gangrene. What had I to do with his misfortune? Nothing, and nothing more than any other person who might have passed him by on the street. But I took the time to listen to him, for he was bowed down by distress, whereas for the first time in years, I felt light and free.

The man needed money, of course. Enough to feed his family while he recovered from the operation. Twenty days wasn't that long. Someone important had promised him help but at the last moment had shut the door in his face. He showed me his rotting leg.

"You're in luck, my friend," I said. "I'm rich."

I gave him five hundred dollars, a sum I would have been

incapable of offering to anyone had the check from my tormentors not been at the bottom of my purse. Twenty years of prison in order to be able, one day, to help an unhappy man hang on for twenty more days . . . Neither of us was really the better for the money changing hands: never again would he have his leg, nor I my youth. But he would not be reduced to begging, to humiliating himself before passersby, to squinting through the tinted windows of Mercedeses, looking for a glimmer of kindness in the passengers' eyes.

Money heals nothing, though it can take the edge off pain. Only one thing in all the world has the power to heal: love—however corny, however predictable that seems. I mean Eric's love, of course, which I've received like a transfusion, refreshing the very blood that beats in my heart. But also the love of my family and friends, all those who with their closeness, warmth, and support have helped me chase away the ghosts.

My family will always be there, and always be strong, even if we're now scattered across the four corners of the earth. We are everlastingly linked by our common trials. We're a bit like the branches of a great tree, reaching out from a trunk that, scarred yet enduring, represents our shared pain, our past, and our identity. Had we been separated during those dark years, none of us would have survived.

Since our liberation in 1991, my mother has struggled with infinite patience (prison is a great teacher of patience) to reclaim our family pride. What happened to our possessions? All the legal traces went up in smoke when the Commander of the Faithful gave the order to demolish our house, believing he could even efface every memory of us. My mother carries on her fight less for herself than for the rest of us. Since the beginning, we've been the only reason this woman, whose life stopped at the age of thirty-six, had to keep on living. Since the beginning, she has carried us all in her arms, trying even when we were cast into Hell to provide us with a childhood worthy of the name. Today the woman who will remain in the eyes of the world "the Widow Oufkir" divides her time between Paris and Marrakesh. She's sixty-nine and can finally allow herself to rest. I know she takes things slowly these days, savoring life as she so richly deserves.

Myriam is also married and lives in Paris, a free woman, but her body bears the traces of her imprisonment. Because of her fragile health, I still help her care for her daughter, Nawal. A real fighter, Myriam hasn't given up trying. After getting her degree as an educational psychologist (an awful name for people who help at-risk children), she's working on a collection of photos to be accompanied by her own poems. For me, her real masterpiece remains Nawal.

Raouf is forty-seven. . . . already! I can hardly believe he's the father of a little girl of twelve. If it didn't sound so pompous, I'd call him the intellectual of the family. More than a mere thinker, he has a collection of academic degrees and is still working on his doctorate. In 2003 in France he published a striking book, *Les Invités* (*The Guests*), in which he revisits the sources of our ordeal. I admire my brother and the strength of character that has driven him ever onward in his thirst for knowledge.

If I'm free today, it's also and above all thanks to Maria. I don't call her a saint for nothing. Thanks to her escape from Morocco in 1996, and to the tumult she unleashed upon her arrival in France, the wall of silence finally fell. She shook the free world, which suddenly stirred from its torpor. Without her, I would definitely still be a phantom of the system, half-free, without a home or a proper job, living on the meager handouts of my tormentors.

My sister is not only a saint, but the mother of a thirteen-year-old boy and the intrepid founder of a film production company. Maria's quite modest and doesn't like to talk about herself, but if she did, there'd be a lot to say.

This family portrait would not be complete without my little artist, my sister Soukaina, who quickly made up for her time in jail by passing her baccalauréat in 1996 and studying law, a subject that hardly seemed suited to her free spirit. Painting, drawing, sculpting—all these were second nature to her, unlike the free world's favorite activity: working in an airless office. Living by her wits and a string of petty jobs, she wandered for a while in search of herself. Today she sings professionally. I love her voice, her style, the lyrics she writes, and I'm not her only admirer: the critics have praised her enthusiastically, and one even claimed that this petite young woman has a bit of Piaf in her!

My brother Abdellatif is the one among us who's had the

hardest time making a new start. Perhaps going to prison as a three-year-old is a burden the rest of us can never fully comprehend. In jail, he grew to love the open sky with a passion, and for a long time harbored hopes of becoming a pilot. He took flying lessons but was unable to continue for financial reasons. I hope he finds his footing, and inner peace as well, for I know what weighs on his soul, because it has taken me so many years to set my own spirit free.

How can any of us ever forget the woman who chose to share the fate of a family whom everyone else had abandoned? Achoura, my mother's cousin, who followed us to the depths of hell, today remains at the heart of our family. The children call her Mamie. I believe she has found happiness. Even if she'll never be as carefree as the world around her, she has found the serenity that for people like us is a true treasure.

Eric's love renews me; the love of my family keeps me whole. My friends, who came little by little into my life, taught me, without seeming to, how to live in the world. It all seems so long ago now, those days of dinner parties when, paralyzed, I wondered how to join in the conversation, and even why I should. Today, my friends are the very air I breathe, people without whom the world would still be an inhospitable place where I would cower in Eric's shadow. The people of the free world are no longer anonymous; they have names: Natalie, Maurice, Nadia, Martin, Suzy, Walid, Tui, Serge, Axel, Cosima,

Beth, Myriam, Claudia, Béatrice, Elisabeth, Laurent, Philippe, Virginie, Wally, Daniel, Brigitte and Daniel, Farid, Baby, Oscar, Carol, Rima, Christian, Vanessa, Ivan . . . And I have so many more friends in France, Morocco, Lebanon, Australia, America, and other countries besides. I'm no longer an explorer in a foreign land. I'm no longer the woman whose entire world was her little family, huddled at the bottom of a hole. I've learned to love, to be loved, to open myself to others. I've learned that they're not so bad, these mysterious people of the free world—quite the opposite, in fact. Sometimes they are even vital to my happiness, and I to theirs, for at long last I know how to give the kind the love I've been so lucky to receive.

ACKNOWLEDGMENTS

I would like to thank the entire staff at Miramax Books. Also, I'm grateful to Jonathan Burnham, Lynn Nesbit, Olivier Nora, and Manuel Carcassonne for their support.